To Le Hoa
From Bernadette with love.

I DREAMT I DWELT IN MARBLE HALLS

Bernadette M Redmond

© Bernadette M Redmond

ISBN-13-978-1491263778

ISBN-10-1491263776

Dedicated to John Redmond and Julia Byrne, my grandparents, and their decent hardworking neighbours and friends who lived in the Artisans' Dwellings, Upper Buckingham Street, Dublin

Table of contents

1. Neither Fish nor Fowl nor Good Red Herring
2. The Granda
3. Our Culchie Roots
4. The Gran
5. The Butchers Boy who never went to War
6. The Bombing of the North Strand
7. The Dwellings
8. Dublineze
9. The Da
10. Faded Glory
11. The Ma
12. Mind Me Domes
13. Awful Times
14. In sickness and in health
15. The Nuns
16. A Penny for the Black Babies
17. Men in Black
18. Cootes and Herons

19. Deck the Halls

20. Credo in Unum Deum

21. For Whom the Bell Tolls.

22. Dya want yer auld lobby washed down

23. Nymphs and Shepherds

24. The Mot

25. The Ciotóg

26. Exodus

Chapter 1
Neither Fish nor Fowl nor Good Red Herring.

'Down in the valley where the green grass grows
there sat 'Bridie' pretty as a rose.
She sang, and she sang and she sang so sweet
'til along came 'Tommy', and kissed her on the cheek.
How many kisses did she get, she aint tellin but we can guess
1, 2, 3, 4....

The Square behind Buckingham Buildings more familiarly known as 'The Dwellings' was splashed with playing children, the boys competing in a game of handball on the back wall of the two cottages facing Bella Street, the girls, plaits and ribbons bobbing, concentrating on the intricacies of a skipping game. Looking out the barred first floor half landing window of Block 'B' I had a bird's eye view of the scene, but even if I hadn't, the names mentioned would have identified the skipping girl, and the boy they were tormenting. The sounds echoed up the stairwell through the eight window apertures between landings which were open to the elements. Annoyed by the skipping rhyme the boys retaliated with

'Down in the valley where the green grass grows
there sat Bridie picking her nose.
She picked, and she picked and she picked so deep
'til along came Tommy and punched her on the cheek.
How many punches did she get, she aint tellin but we can guess
1, 2, 3, 4....

In the mid forties and until the advent of more fearful times, we were children of the streets with our own game rules and rhymes, jeers and jokes, mnemonics and rites, slang and secret spells, all sucked in by osmosis to be remembered for a life time. Upper Buckingham Street and Lower Rutland Street formed the east and west boundaries of our world while Summerhill and Lower Gloucester Street, now Lower Seán Mc Dermott Street, formed north and south. Being more or less traffic free Bella Street was our right of way from Lower Rutland Street through to Upper Buckingham Street so we took possession and claimed it as our own. Summerhill Place, formerly a mews full of coach houses backing on to the grand Regency houses on Summerhill, also ran between both Streets but mostly consisted of sheds, stables and pig yards along the left hand side. These had metamorphosed from the coach houses, and irate owners did not encourage kids to hang about, quite apart from the fact that the smell of manure in warm weather was eye watering. But our sanctum of sanctums was 'The Square'. As you entered its sloped entrance from Bella Street it had a flight of steps on the left up to the Terrace where we learned to walk along the balustraded wall balancing twelve foot above the Square, a strictly forbidden activity but one at which we all became proficient. The end of the Terrace had an exit to Summerhill Place and was a discrete way of crossing Buckingham Street to the Pawn or to procure Penny Dinners from the local soup kitchen in the basement of Lourdes House. Below the Terrace were the Arches where we used to scourge the elderly occupants by playing in the shelter they afforded on a wet day. Unlike the unforgiving concrete covered Square the Arches had a nice smooth tarmac floor ideal for drawing 'beds', playing hop scotch and skating. Continuing clockwise in the Square were about eight artisan cottages and then, facing the Terrace, the back entrances to the basement flats in the three blocks of our

Artisan Dwellings. To complete the square was the back wall of the two cottages facing Bella Street. Thoughtfully built with no windows facing the Square it had a goal post outlined in chalk, and a bigger higher chalked outline set for games of handball. This wall was claimed by the boys, usually without contention, but sometimes the girls would make a stand and take it over for 'two ball'.

I have read best seller books on life in the tenements around Summerhill and the Gloucester Diamond and find them too depressing for words. The deprivation and depravity described is probably more descriptive of an earlier turn of the century timeline so was as foreign to me as it was to all the decent families I knew who brought up their children in dire poverty in these streets. While at times their children may have been cold and hungry, and may not have had money for material possessions they provided solid stable homes which few of their children would judge inadequate. So Dear Reader if you're expecting self pitying narration you're reading the wrong book.

'Don't sue your readers for sympathy,' the great American Essayist Phillip Lopate advises. Well there's no fear of that here! This is but a slice of neighbourhood and family life in our own little ghetto. We were poor but 'klane and dacent'.

As children we didn't choose our friends by their home conditions although having a Ma or a Gran who was good for a jam sandwich, or bread spread with dripping, was a definite advantage. More important was their availability to come out to play. The endless freedom of the streets was, to some degree, curtailed for kids like us who went to the nuns at William St. School. We fared less favourably than the chislers who went to the nearer Rutland St School because we had homework to complete, the nuns believing the Devil made work for idle minds, while the teachers at Rutland St were out the door on the first sound of the bell and were certainly not going to waste their evenings correcting exercise books. Another consideration when asking somebody out to play was what equipment they possessed, depending on what game or activity was in vogue e.g. a piece of stick or cap gun for cowboys and Indians, a polish tin for playing hop scotch, chestnuts for conkers, marbles, jackstones, a few coppers for pitch and toss, an old tie for blind man's bluff, a rolled up newspaper for 'Are you there Mori-ar-ity', a deck of cards for pontoon, 21's or snap, tennis balls for handball or two ball, an empty can for kick the can, an old bicycle wheel and stick to use as a hoop, thread for knock-knock, a bat for rounder's, and most prized of all, a football or a rope long enough for multiple skipping or swinging on lamp posts. Nothing at all was needed for 'Folly the leader' or Relieve-o apart from speed at running away, and all that was require for Statues was patience. But the crème de la crème mucker was the possessor of a box car for zooming down Lower Rutland Street or the more dangerous hill in Upper Buckingham Street.

Mostly boys and girls played separately, with the boys being quite clear about what games they would, and would not participate in, but for all their pickiness even the poorest kids could participate in those games. I was cursed with having to look after my brother, Seán, so he learned how to play with the girls whether he liked it or not. He became quite proficient at skipping and two ball, and by the time he was six or seven, and big enough to be trusted to play with other boys I should have been able to get rid of him, but *my* friends would come calling for him if they were short of somebody to turn the rope. I'd be listening, waiting for them to ask Gran if I could abandon my homework and come out to play, but bold as brass I'd hear them ask 'Can Seán come out'? They, at least called him 'Seán'. He was known by the local gurriers as Gik-Gik because of the big brown birthmark on the calf of his leg. His compatriots in the Dwellings had equally expressive street names and were forever after known as Chancer, Boxey, Gameball, Wobbler, Combo and Ra-Ra. There was also a miniature Jimmy Cagney who was known as Shugs which changed to Shags as he reached puberty.

Swinging on lamp posts was regarded as an act of vandalism by the Polis so younger kids were rewarded for keeping 'cavo' by being allowed a go. Being caught by Sgt. Jeremiah Sullivan from Store Street was a terrifying experience. He marched me off home one day to tangle with Granda.

'Do ye own dis child' said the Sergeant his big ham of a fist encasing my scrawny neck?

'Niver seen that yung wan before in me life' retorted Granda, barring the Sergeant's progress. Gran came to the door and rescued me while the Sergeant explained my heinous crime.

'Well to put it in a nutshell Sergeant' said a grim faced Granda, rocking on his heels and fingers stuck in braces to prevent himself thumping him for laying hands on me 'yiz are probably used to raising sheep where youze come from, but round about here we earn peanuts so we rear monkeys, and since we don't have any trees, the little feckers use the lamp posts, so we're banjacksed'.

The big Cork man looked at him in confusion and left blustering about his sworn duty to prevent damage to Corporation property. His chief annoyance was that while chasing me my fellow law breakers had managed to rescue the precious rope with whipped ends that had lashed Guinness barrels in a former life. He used to roar at us after that but he never went near the Granda again. I think he saw the glint of reckoning in his eyes.

My brother Seán and my sister Bridie and I disappeared each summer to spend eight week's with my mother's family in Claregalway a townland in Co. Galway. Country children broke up two weeks earlier than City so we were not marked absent on the last two week of the summer term at William St. on the understanding that we would be improving our Irish down in the Gaeltacht. We didn't of course we just ran wild for the extra two weeks and came back to Dublin looking like tinkers children, covered in briar scratches and calluses on our feet from going without shoes. On our return to the streets we would always have to earn our way back to acceptance as new allegiances would have been forged during our absence. Being gone for two months we missed out on Dublin at its best. With Dollymount strand, the Royal Canal, Phoenix Park and the mountains on their doorstep local kids enjoyed what these places had to offer, at little or no cost. Boys in particular, ranged far and wide doing things their Mammies never knew about, but that their Daddies suspected, having once been little gurriers themselves, so, for example, while they scrounged the entrance fee to the 'Baths' from their Ma, their Da would look at the togs under their arm and glare at them, growling a *'Youze be careful'*, knowing full well they were off to the 'Locks', but hoping that their sense of self preservation was as good as their swimming.

Chapter 2

The Granda

The Dublin Artisans' Dwelling Company, under the chairmanship of Sir Edward Cecil Guinness completed their Buckingham Street Dwellings in 1876. Designed by Thomas Drew they were four stories high over basement flats. The entrances to the basement flats were accessed from the Square to the rear. The rest of the block had three entrances with central stairs for each entrance. There were four flats off each landing, with a bolted door giving access to the landings, which were of generous proportions and well kept, cleaning being the joint responsibility of each four tenants. The rent, at 3s.6p a dwelling was relatively high, even for skilled workers, and was beyond the means of labourer's who earned about a £1 a week.

John Redmond, my grandfather, born in Stradbally, Co. Laois in 1876 moved a wife and two children in sometime before the birth of their daughter, Sheila, in 1921. Since his marriage to Julia Byrne in 1906 they had lived a hand to mouth existence in rooms rented around Sheriff Street district, known in the early 18th century, as the North Dublin Lotts. The area lay on reclaimed land between the Tolka and the Liffey rivers with the principal streets named after their makers; Commons, Mayor, Sherriff and Guild, the latter bisected by the Royal Canal as it joined the Liffey at the North Wall. By mid 18th century it all became part of the Viscount Mountjoy's Estate. Luke Gardiner aka the First Viscount Mountjoy, fell, leading the County of Dublin Militia at the battle at New Ross in the 1798 Rebellion. His son, Charles John Gardiner inherited large swathes of Regency Dublin but died from apoplexy aged forty six in 1816, predeceased by his only heir, Luke William Gardiner. The Estate collapsed during the famine years, creating some of the worst tenements in Dublin, but keeping an affordable roof over my grandparent's heads for nearly sixteen years. The First Viscount was one of the few of his heritage to champion Catholic Emancipation.

Granda Redmond had been involved in the bitter Dublin Lockout of 1913-4, and his political affiliations made him unemployable for long periods of time. William Martin Murphy, Chairman of the *Dublin United Tram Company's* dismissal of 200 tramway men ignited what would become the most infamous dispute in Irish labour history the Lockout of the tramway men and the industrial strife that grew out of it. It was always going to be an unequal struggle for, as the workers were soon to learn to their cost, the employers could rely on the forces of the state to back up their position. Foremost among the employers opposed to trade unionism in Ireland was William Martin Murphy. A highly successful businessman from Co Cork in 1913, as well as being the *Chairman of the Dublin United Tramway Company* he was owner of *Clery's Department Store* and the *Imperial Hotel*. He also had a controlling interest in the *Irish Independent, Evening Herald* and *Irish Catholic* newspapers and was a major shareholder in the *B and I Ferry* Line.

James Larkin's arrival in Ireland as Organiser for the National Union of Dock Labourers inspired dockers like Granda to unite. Disagreement with the NUDL's Liverpool Executive led to Larkin's suspension and the launch in 1909 of a Dublin-based union for unskilled workers - the Irish Transport and General Workers' Union. Larkin advocated refusing to handle 'tainted goods' from companies involved in the Lockout. Murphy as Head of the Employers Federation was intent upon breaking the power of the ITGWU, so set out to annihilate its leaders. To achieve this all workers of Federation Employers had to sign the following declaration if they wanted to keep their jobs

'I hereby undertake to carry out all instructions given to me by or on behalf of my employers and further I agree to immediately resign my membership of the Irish Transport and General Workers Union (if a member) and I further undertake that I will not join or in any way support this union.

Nearly 30,000 workers, including Granda, with a wife and young children, refused, so a total Lockout of all strikers was enforced by employer's in August and by the middle of October their families faced up to the prospect of a bleak winter with inadequate warmth or nourishment and dependent on charity and food parcels from Trade Unionists across in Liverpool. It was in this climate of desperation, intimidation and conflict that a plan was proposed to send the children of striking workers, like the Da and his brother Martin, to England to ensure their survival. They were probably too young to go anyway but the Catholic Church's vociferous opposition to sending Dublin children to a Heathen Country ensured that the scheme foundered and by January, when it was obvious that the TUC in England would not come out in sympathy, the strike was over. The capitulation for thousands of workers and their families left them destitute. Although the Lockout was lifted strikers could not now get work as they were blacklisted by employers. For the employers, on the other hand, and particularly for William Martin Murphy, who had always seen Larkinism as the embodiment of radicalism and disruption, nothing less than the avoidance of a social revolution had been achieved. Larkin defeated, left for America.

Although Granda continued to work on the Docks, when he was lucky enough to get a 'Tally' in the daily lottery, he never got his Button. In time, with the Irish Free State Treaty in its infancy he acquired a job with the Lighterhouse Company, working as a

Fireman on Liffey tugboats. Earning £3.6s a week and, with a surety from his Employer that he could pay the rent, he was granted a tenancy at 31 Buckingham Buildings, Upper Buckingham Street the official Post Office address of the Artisans' Dwellings.

Most of the street names in the area were inherited from the British aristocracy that had laid claim to them; Amien, Buckingham, Clarence, Gardiner, Gloucester, Marlborough, Rutland and Talbot being a few. The Wide Streets Commission of 1751 at the start of the Georgian period ensured that our northside streets were broad, unlike the narrow winding mediaeval streets of the old city mostly on the south side of the Liffey. They became a fit setting for terraces and squares full of elegant houses. Summerhill, the main artery of our neighbourhood, with a shop to meet everybody's need, was originally Summer Hill, and before that Farmers Hill, the summer residence of Luke, Viscount Gardiner, the First. The grand Regency Houses on the eastern side were built in the last decade of the eighteenth century and housed other members of Burkes Peerage such as the Ffrenches, the Duke of Portland and the Viscount's Buckingham and Rutland. Like the Gardiner Estate they disintegrated into tenements and are now demolished.

One of my Grandfather's favourite records was a rendition of 'The Bohemian Girl' which contained the song 'I dreamt that I dwelt in Marble Halls, with vassals and serfs at my side'. 'Well Jools' he used to say 'The Artisans Dwelling Company might not have been able to deck their halls with marble, but nobody can say they stinted on the size, they're nearly as big as the bloody flat'.

Chapter 3
Our Culchie Roots

Granda was the fifth of seven children born on the Cosby Estate. His parents Martin Redmond and Mary Higgins were also born in Laois, known in their era, as the Queens County. On the 1901 Census he had moved to Dublin and was living with his widowed mother in Irishtown in Dublin. In 1903 he married a young dressmaker, Mary Ellen Melia from Lower Sherriff Street. They found rooms nearby and settled down to married life, but their happiness was short lived. Mary Ellen died from tuberculosis on the 15th of February 1905, age twenty four years, twelve days after she gave birth to a daughter, Annie.

Although Sir Charles Cameron, the underrated Chief Health and Medical Officer of Dublin had reduced the death rate among Dublin's poor by a quarter between 1901 and 1911 when more families had lived in dire poverty in one room in crumbling tenements, and with higher death rates, than in any other City in the United Kingdom. While more than half the deaths in Dublin occurred in the tenements the two Poor Houses, Asylums and other Institutions were recorded as the last resting place of 41.9%. For pregnant women it was probably scant consolation to know that you stood more chances of dying of puerperal fever in the City's Lying in Hospital's than you did if you delivered in the Poor House.

Eighteen months later on the 4th. of November 1906 John's period of mourning ended when he married Julia Byrne, my grandmother, a seamstress, age twenty four years, in St. Lawrence O'Toole Church, Seville Place.

Julia was the oldest of six children of William Byrne and Mary Quinn, the Byrne family having reared six generations of children in the Liberties. The Gran's family was close knit, apart from Alice, who did not fit comfortably into her environment. Gran used to describe her as 'dawny' or 'not the full shilling'.

Out of nine pregnancies Gran and Granda raised four children, Peter, my father, born 1909, Martin 1912, Sheila 1921 and Tess 1925. My father, Peter, produced three children, myself, Bridie and Seán; Martin's wife Lucy had six, Jackie, Anthony, Stanley, Kenneth, Martin and Neville. Sheila, married to Christy Clinton, had Éamon, Carol and Bernard, and Tess wed to Tommy Flynn, had Bernadette and Denise.

By the time I was born my grandparents had lived through the Boer War, the Great Lockout, WWI, the Easter Rising, the War of Independence and Civil War, the latter leading to *Saorstát Éireann*, the transition to an Irish Free State in 1922. The Irish Free State came to an end in 1937 the year before my birth, when the citizens voted by referendum to replace the 1922 constitution. It was succeeded by the sovereign and current state of Ireland, which until 1949 was often referred to as Eire.

Bullet holes from the Black and Tans Gatling gun's strafing the Buildings in 1921 remained as a memento of their reign of terror throughout my childhood. My birth in December 1938 heralded the likelihood of another war despite Clement Atlee's hope of 'Peace in our time', and so it happened that WW2 began in September 1939. For the next six years Eire became a neutral state as we lived through 'The Emergency' as De Valera euphemistically called it. Censorship of news and letters began followed by rationing and internment. I learned from an early age not to mention the name deValera aka 'the Devil's spawn, and son of an American trollop and a Spanish hoor in Granda's hearing. His description of somebody as a hoor usually denoted male and clever and was usually preceded by the word 'cute'.

The only hoor that was preceded by the word 'bastard' was the Blessed Matt Talbot, a local blackleg and saint in the making who had lived in lodgings at 18 Upper Rutland Street.

I have no idea what he thought when Sheila named her first child 'Éamon', but he never held it against the lad and once Éamon was old enough to walk any distance he used to take him on his meanders down the Quay.

I didn't know any of Granda's siblings but vaguely remember some of them at his funeral in 1949. They remained just names to me, Kate, Mary Anne, Michael, Elizabeth, Margaret and Patrick. Annie, his daughter by Mary Ellen, also came to his funeral. She had joined the WAAF during the WW2, returning home in 1946 so I knew she was part of the family. I had assumed she had been raised by her mother's parents, but discovered, when I started compiling a family tree that there was no sign of Annie in the family on the 1911 Census so the childhood of little Orphan Annie remains a mystery. However I recently traced her death certificate to Old Trafford in England and evidence that she had remained in contact with Martin and his family.

Chapter 4

The Gran

Jackeen to the core Gran was born in the Liberties, the area south of the Liffey, outside the Medieval City Walls, where William Byrne, a printer, my paternal great grandfather, was born in 1857. He married Mary Quinn, age twenty, whose family came from around Herberton Bridge in Dolphins Barn. They married in 1881 in St James's Chapel, and moved out of the Liberties, finding lodgings on the north side of the Liffey. No.19 Upper Dominick Street had been the Regency house of William O'Kelly MD. Of course Dr O'Kelly, his family and servants had long moved on, and No.19 was now a multi occupied grandiose tenement, albeit with a closed hall door. Six of Mary's seven children survived and moved on from there over to the Gardiner Estate area.

Julia, aka Jools, my grandmother, the oldest, worked as a box maker when she left school and was then apprenticed to a dressmaker and became a skilled seamstress. She may well have been apprenticed to Granda's first wife Mary Ellen, a dressmaker, who lived next door. Marion also worked in a box factory and suffered from progressive deafness, Joe became a printer like his father, Alice appears to have been 'beyond parental control' and spent most of her life in Institutional settings, dying in the South Dublin Poor House, Billy was a butcher's boy having failed to join the Dublin Fusiliers and was a mine of information on esoteric subjects. Kitty married late in life so was childless. She moved Marion and Billy into her home in Ringsend when her husband, Tom, died. Before their move Marion and Billy, and their widowed mother, Mary, had done the rounds of the Gardiner Estate, ending up in 1 Rutland Cottages around the corner from Gran in the Dwellings in Upper Buckingham Street. They were a scrawny little family but they all saw in their three score and ten.

Despite their rickety appearance some of their previous generation had been deemed fit enough to take the 'King's Shilling' and lie in unmarked graves across the African veldt and at Suvla and Sud el Bhar. Apart from far off Commonwealth graves the only places to commemorate their memory is the Fusiliers Arch at St. Stephens Green and a memorial in Glasnevin.

Several times a year Granda had a glorious day to himself when Gran took us over to Ringsend on the tram to spend the day with her siblings. Kitty always made caraway seed cake, Marion desperately tried to hear what we said to her, and Billy would take us along to Sandymount Strand on a fine day, or invite us in to his back yard shed on a wet one to play Pontoon or Cribbage. His shed was like a little snug with an old armchair, a few bockety stools, small table and a primus. Having no great liking for caraway seed cake Billy used to make us his specialty, buttered bread sprinkled with cocoa and sugar. It was years before I wondered *why* he had had a garden shed when he had no garden, and to the best of my recollection, never grew anything. I suppose it was his little retreat from his sisters

Joe, the older of Grans two brothers, lived on Clonliffe Avenue, and dropped into the Gran's occasionally and was always good for a sixpenny piece. I never met his wife Evelyn or children.

'Comes from a family who didn't have a pot to piss in, and now thinks she's Queen of the May' was the Gran's sagacious opinion of Evelyn.

We used to call Uncle Joe 'Gawny Mac' because no matter what news you gave him his response would be 'Gawny Mac is that a fact' with the sound of wonderment in his voice.

Gran's early married life was hard, and with Granda not having the security of 'the Button' to give him the status of a regular dock worker I believe she had, at times, to resort to charitable organizations for help. Her attitude to organized charities was such that it was most likely formed by bitter experience and conflict. The St Vincent de Paul and Infant Aid Societies and Lourdes House, known as the 'Buckingham Street Dinner House' worthy as they might have been, were anathema to her. Apart from the Quakers, the denominational nature of Charities in Ireland meant that workers who espoused Marxists or radical leanings were given a hard time. The spectre of Communism loomed large so both the Catholic and Church of Ireland hierarchies ensured that charitable and welfare services were under their control, and Diocesan clergy were judged to be the most appropriate people to engage in this work. Distribution of funds was often delegated to committees or gobshites, which, for some was too bitter a pill to swallow so many poor people, depended on the pawnbroker for survival.

Gran never crossed their doorstep and I thought she would drop dead on the spot when she saw me coming out of the local premises one day having redeemed Jim Fitzpatrick's Sunday suit for Irene. Pawnbrokers were not as avaricious as the money lenders, who were despised. The former was limited by law to an interest rate of 5d per £1 per month, while the latter' usually a woman, could charge any amount of interest on her loans, 50% was not uncommon. The other alternative was the Tallyman's never-never schemes which often ended in midnight flits.

Julia Byrne was a frugal thrifty woman who always seemed to be able to provide food and fuel, and pay the rent and her penny policies. Because of her parsimoniousness I used to be mortified going shopping along Summerhill with her. I always think of her attitude to measured meted out charity whenever I read the words of John Boyle O'Reilly

The organized charity, scrimped and iced,
in the name of a cautious statistical Christ.
The smile restrained the respectable cant
when a friend in need is a friend in want.
When the only aim is to keep afloat
and a brother may die with a cry in his throat.

Chapter 5

The Butchers Boy who never went to War

Billy Byrne's most prized possession was a ring made from a small nugget of South African gold inherited from an uncle who had served in the Dublin Fusiliers during the Boer War. Billy, born in 1889, had tried to join the Regiment during WW1. His first attempt at fifteen got his ears boxed by his irate mother Mary who also threatened to emasculate the Fusiliers Recruitment Sergeant unless he tore up the form Billy had signed. Billy had already taken 'the King's Shilling' by completing the form filling process, with the Recruiting Sergeant claiming his fee of sixpence for signing him up. Billy, the volunteer, had then gone home, and but for the intervention of his Ma would have received his joining instructions and travel warrant a day or two later. No proof of age was asked for nor, proof of identity, but you had to be 5'3" and pass a cursory medical. As far as the Army was concerned you were who you said you were. On reaching eighteen he tried his luck with the Royal Irish Regiment, and according to Billy, was rejected on health grounds. Billy's version was it was because of his poor eye sight; Gran's mocking explanation was that it was because of his flat feet. Billy's mammy almost certainly saved him from certain death. I don't know how many Byrnes joined the Irish Regiments but 297 of them died on WW1 battlefields, or of the wounds or gassing they sustained in action.

Billy worked all his life as a butchers 'boy'. He was small and wiry riding a bike nearly as big as himself. When a Butcher recruited a 'boy' the standard joke advertisement in their shop window read; *BOY WANTED. MUST BE BUILT AS BIG AS A PRAM TO PUSH A BIKE AS BIG AS A TRAM*

When he went to collect his old age pension he discovered the differential between his entitlement and his wages was a mere 18s/6d.

He once took me to the partially built War Memorial out at Island Bridge and lamented the fact that despite it being post WW2 we still had not commemorated Irelands fifty thousand fallen on the Western Front battlefields during WW1. How right he was when he said Ireland would never see its completion during DeValera's, anti British lifetime and his blind indifference to the deaths of those who thought they would achieve Home Rule by joining the British Army. It is Irelands shame that the price they paid was never acknowledged and that they were air brushed out of history. They were never seen as young men who understood the concepts of honour and duty, and having been taught right from wrong went to the aid of Belgium and Alsace-Lorraine because the cause was a just one. With small nations being threatened by a Prussian Empire the only way they could do this was to fight with the British Empire, an Empire that had (at last) granted Home Rule for Ireland. Home Rule had been the aspiration of Irish nationalists for fifty years and, finally, in 1914 it appeared that the deed was done. On 18 September 1914 the Third Irish Home Rule Bill became law, although its implementation was suspended for the duration of war which had been declared on August 4th. The fact that the Bill was passed at all was due to the tenacity of Herbert Henry Asquith the last Prime Minister of the United Kingdom to lead a purely Liberal Party cabinet. His importance in Irish history is that he succeeded in enacting the Bill after Gladstone's failures of 1886 and 1893.

However the opposition of the Unionists, the outbreak of the WW1 and the fact that by May 1915 Asquith had to form a coalition government between his Liberal Party, the Labour Party and the Tories, including Sir Edward Carson as Attorney-General saw to it that it was never implemented. Appointing Carson to the Cabinet was much to the alarm of John Redmond Leader of the Home Rule Party who had also been urged to become a minister in the new cabinet by Asquith but felt he must continue to support it from outside, in accordance with the Irish Nationalist policy of not accepting government office. Asquith's leadership of the coalition Cabinet was further weakened by the 1916 Easter Rising which resulted in the weasel Lloyd George gaining the support of Bonar Law and the Tories, and forced him to resign as Prime Minister by the end of the year. He bitter criticism of Lloyd George's Irish policy was of 'giving to Ulster a Parliament which it did not want, and to the remaining three-quarters of Ireland a Parliament which it would not have'. Some would say that John Redmond was naïve in his strategy and trust in the fair-mindedness of the British Liberal Party under Lloyd George, with whom he now shared power in a Parliamentary coalition, but it was not one about which he had a lot of choice. He was unbelievably cursed in that everything that possibly could go wrong went wrong. WW1, mobilisation of militant resistance to Home Rule in Ulster supported and sustained by the leaders of the Conservative Party, an Irish rebellion, the death of his brother at the Front and a proposal to impose conscription in Eire supervened in the six-year interval between the introduction of the Home Rule Bill and his death on March 6th, 1918.

On June 7, 1917, his brother Major Willie Redmond MP for East Clare was killed in action while leading the Royal Irish Brigade to victory at the Battle of Messines Ridge, at Ypres, Belgium. It was a devastating blow. A member of the Irish Party, he had represented East Clare for 25 years at Westminster. At 53 years old he was too old to be a soldier, but like John he was convinced that an Ireland, loyal to the Crown, would succeed in achieving Home Rule, and so he joined the Irish troops in Flanders. At least neither of them was around to see De Valera inherit the East Clare Parliamentary seat or to see the carnage of the Civil War that followed when brother killed brother in the name of nationhood

Dev's vindictive treatment of WW2 soldiers who had transferred from the neutral Free State Army to British Regiments to fight Fascism was equally brutal. This spiteful treatment was continued by Costello and his Fine Gael party which took power from Dev and Fianna Fáil in 1948. There has been much historical debate regarding the extent to which the Irish Blueshirts, and by extension Fine Gael and Costello himself, had ties to European fascist movements pre and post war, and speculation on the extent of their desire for a German victory. Some of these WW2 Irishmen had taken part in major campaigns and sea battles but on their return to Ireland were treated like lepers and put on a special list with their names circulated to every Government Department, Town Hall and other possible locations where they may have sought work. For those who had given their lives their widows and children were appallingly treated by local authorities leaving them little choice but to immigrate and seek refuge in a more humane society. It would take until 1986, eleven years after De Valera's death, for a National Day of Commemoration to be agreed that would not only remember Republicans, and those who died on UN peace-keeping missions abroad with the Irish Defence Forces, but also Irishmen who fought in WWI and WW2 with the British Army and Navy.

Like a lot of people Billy didn't leave much of a mark on the world and doesn't have a headstone to honour his passing. If he had it should read

'Fear no more the heat o' th' sun nor the furious winter rages;
Thou thy worldly task hast done, home art gone and ta'en thy wages.
(Source; Shakespeare; Cymbeline)

Chapter 6

The Bombing of the North Strand.

The North Strand Road got its name from the fact that it was originally under the waters of the Liffey at the mouth Dublin Bay at high tide. It was reclaimed as part of the 1717 North Dublin Lotts and became a thoroughfare between Fairview Park and Amien Street Station. I remember the bombing. It is unlikely that this is a true memory but it is a very vivid and detailed one. I was only two and a half at the time and as **memory is malleable and shifts over time this one is probably constructed by combining actual events with family reminiscences.** I say this because for years I thought the bombing had taken place later in the war, and that I must have been older, but history records that it happened on 31st May 1941.

Dubliners recount it as the bombing of the North Strand the bombs fell in a crescent shape, dropping on Newcomen Court, Clarence Street, Empress Place, Rutland Place, and Summerhill Parade and finally Upper Buckingham Street on their way out. The bombs in Empress Place and numbers 3-4 Upper Buckingham rocked Buckingham Buildings to its foundations. My parents lived further up Summerhill in Upper Rutland Street so we only heard the explosions and saw the glow of subsequent fires.

Twenty nine people died, ninety were injured and three hundred houses destroyed or damaged. We, the citizens of Rutland Street, were woken up around midnight by the air raid siren on the roof of the Oifig an Phoist Depot on Summerhill and the beams of the Costal Defense Watch searchlights piercing the darkness for the Vickers 3.7 Anti Air Craft Battery in Clontarf to strafe the sky in response to reports of aircraft travelling up the East coast. The

ARP warden was banging on neighbours doors to get everybody down to the shelter in the middle of Rutland Street. Granda, being a member of the AFB, was on duty to cut off supplies of gas, water and electricity to damaged building, put out small fires, tackle incendiaries and render first aid was doing an equally thankless task down in Buckingham Street. Living in a neutral country most families ignored them so we were practically the only people in the Rutland Street shelter, because nobody really believed we would be bombed. We had just gone back to bed on the all clear when all hell let loose. The Belfast Blitz, on the 15th April and the 4th May should have prepared us for the possibility of at least collateral damage. Nearly 900 people died as a result of the first bombing and 1,500 were injured. In terms of property damage, half of the houses in Belfast were damaged or destroyed. In the second raid on the night of Sunday the 4th. May 150 were killed.

The North Strand bombing, I've read, started about 01.30 on the Whit weekend Saturday so my recollection is one of my Ma, Julia Loftus, mother of two, from the bogs of Gortcloonmore in Co. Galway, trying to put my shoes on and doing a lot of shouting, mostly at my Da to close the shutters and get us down to the air raid shelter again. My father, Peter Redmond, eldest son of Granny Redmond, had Bridie, age four months in his arms looking out of our first floor back window. The view through our eight pane expanse of glass was spectacular since we were in a direct line north of the bombing. The skies were being criss crossed by searchlights as the ack-ack guns sprayed empty skies. Smoke and flames and exploding gas rose from the bomb sites at Summerhill Parade, Newcomen Court and the North Strand as my father closed the shutters to protect us from flying glass. We eventually got back to the shelter, clutching our gas masks and with our coats over our night dresses. This time it was packed. I have no recollection how long we were down there, all I remember is the smell of stale pee, and, Mr. Green, who had a stutter giving out the Rosary. It seemed to go on forever, and probably did. All the family escaped unscathed, and much to the chagrin of the local kids both Rutland Street and North William Street Schools remained intact 'tho the fine stained glass windows over the sanctuary area of St. Agatha's Church were blown out. There have been several theories about the bombing, the most persistent being that the Luftwaffe used BBC radio navigation for night bombing because of the difficulty of seeing blacked out targets. Radio navigation used two radio beacons to form an X over a target. It is believed in some quarters that the British transmitted a third beam moving the cross hairs, causing the Luftwaffe to veer away from Belfast or Liverpool and bomb Dublin by mistake. The less charitable believed that Churchill did it deliberately to draw Éire into the war. The RAF were not dependent on radio signals choosing to bomb when weather conditions favoured celestial navigation, a much more accurate method of hitting their target.

Chapter 7
The Dwellings

By the 1940's, and sixty years old, the Artisan Dwellings were commonly called 'the Buildings' by local people although they were still known as the 'Artisans' Dwellings' on the 1939-40 Electoral Rolls.

Families were well established, with some of their children of an age to seek tenancies in their own right. The Dunne's, Breslin's, Grant's, Fitzpatrick's, Foran's, Kelly's, O'Farrell's, McCarthy's, Mulhall's and Walsh's are some that come to mind. At one point a disgruntled prospective tenant suggested that the Artisans' Dwelling Company should rename the site 'Grants Mansions' and be done with it. There may have been some judicious rising of eyebrows, and muttered accusations of favouritism and undue influence about allocations, but apart from the Dunne's and O'Connor's the denizens, on the whole, lived in harmony. It was very much a matriarchal enclave where the women took it in turns to clean their landings and wash down their flight of stairs. They bickered about who had used Annie Lawlor's Jeyes Fluid, who had spilled turf debris all over the stairs, and sin of sins, who had left the landing door unbolted over night. The latter was a service to courting couples wanting a little bit of romance and privacy on their way to their respective beds.

Nick Colgan who lived in No. 25 was employed by the Company to maintain the Dwellings and had the onerous task of painting the walls of the landings and stairwells. The Company chose the colour of the paint, but it was Nick who got the blame for the 'scutter yellow' walls we had to live with for several years. As part of the tenancy agreement balconies facing the street were not allowed to hang clothes out unlike those that faced the Square so part of his job was to enforce the rule which did not enhance his popularity. Small flats, big families and no washing machines left women with three choices for doing the family washing. While anything wringable was hand washed bulky items were taken as 'bag wash' to the local Municipal Wash House where there were facilities for the women to wash, wring and dry, an exhausting and time consuming session. The other choices were to take your bag wash to the local Magdalene Laundry for a wet wash or a dry wash. Gran chose to use the wet option which meant everything was washed; starched, put through mechanical wringers, folded and returned damp dry and ready for ironing. The dry, deluxe service meant they were returned ironed. The only problem with the wet wash option was we had to put up with starched towels which enraged a shaving tender faced Granda. In posher neighbourhoods there was a door to door laundry service supplied by laundries with names like the Swastika and White Swan but their liveried vans never graced Summerhill. Nick, to do him justice, was generous with the use of his handcart to take the sheet, or counterpane wrapped, bundles along Bella Street, down the Bunkey Hill and across to the Magdalene Convent.

The mother's in the Dwellings castigated and cursed each other's children and minded them when necessary. They criticized one another, supported one another, delivered babies when a 'Bona Fide' midwife wasn't available,, or couldn't be afforded, and laid out and waked the dead. They loaned what finery they had for christenings and weddings, and being mindful that they were a bit more fortunate than their neighbours in the tenements on the other side of the street, tried to fulfill as many of the corporal works of mercy as they could.

The crumbling Georgian tenements that faced the Dwellings were some of the worst in Dublin. With gaping hall doors, high ceilings and ornate centre pieces from which chandeliers had hung in grander times they still had a seedy elegance and housed decent families in single rooms, doing their best in dire circumstances, but lacked the security of the Artisans' tenancies and the co-operative way of living engendered by its structure.

Reaching the end of her endurance in one of the tenements Martin Grant's wife, May Donoghue, walked her children across to the Royal Canal and drowned herself and all six children. For years afterwards May was used as a yardstick to gauge somebody's state of mind coping with the stress and strife of daily life 'Well' things are bad, but I'm not as desperate as poor May' they'd say sagaciously. Or when their children were scourging them; 'Suffering Jesus, if youze don't get out from under me feet I'll take yiz all down to the feckin canal and drown yiz'. If a mother had a 'touch of the nagers' neighbours rallied round and offered the family what support they could until she was able to face the world again. Mental illness was poorly understood. Depression was regarded as a luxury the poor couldn't afford, but an attack of nerves or a 'touch of the nagers' as it was euphemistically called was understandable. I remember Annie Lawlor saying of one young neighbour

'Sure the poor woman is drifting around like a witch's ghost'.

Support for men with the nagers was more judgmental because it usually went hand in hand with 'the drink' and family strife.

The dread of the elderly at the time was to die in St.Kevin's Hospital, previously the South Dublin Workhouse, while others, younger and fitter, shrank from incarceration in 'Grangegorman' part prison, part asylum, and nominally a psychiatric hospital. It was a word that was always whispered and said accompanied by the sign of the cross and a sprinkling of Holy Water if a font was to hand.

Chapter 8

Dublineze

It's the mission in life of most children to scourge their parents and to have parental threats heaped on them in return. Being 'called in' from the freedom of the streets always caused 'internecine' strife. I use the Latin source of the word here which translates as fighting all the way to the death.
Mothers or big sisters were experts at shouting death defying threats into the Square from balconies or stair wells;
'If youze value yer life don't bring me down dere',
I'll hang draw and quarter youze if ya don't gerrup here,
or less fatal;
'If youze bring me down dere I'll redden yer arse/ legs/ ears'
or,
'Gerrup here before I scalp youze ya heart scaldin' little maggot'
'Youze are off to Artane in the mornin' if youze don't gerrup dese stairs'
'I'll tell your Da when he gets home and he'll leather your hide', yeh right!
Threats were water off a ducks back and were regarded as part of everyday life. Insults were also part of our childhood but were mostly directed at the young males of the species. Being called a 'gunner eyed git', 'scabby little shoite' snotty nosed guttersnipe, a 'hoor's melt' or 'bockety arsed bowzie' went unremarked because they were said without malice.
Adult verbal obfuscations often confused us and included;
'Shut your gob and ate yer dinner'
'If youze break yer neck, don't come runnin ta me'

'Dya wannit now, or will youze wait 'til yiz get it', and most puzzling of all 'It's up in Nelly's room behind the wallpaper or 'She's minding mice for Mary Ann'.
An exasperated neighbour said to me one day
'Hold on, I'll see if she's up me hole pickin daisy's' when I asked where her daughter was.
Gran thought that was very 'common' and said 'what would you expect from yer wan when 'she's worn a groove across the road' e.g. 'spent her life in the pawnshop'. On the other end of the scale, if somebody was acting above their station her pithy opinion was that 'the higher a monkey climbs the more you see of his arse'. Whenever I was answerable to somebody promoted above their capabilities I saw a red arsed baboon and I'd remember the Gran's judgement. I used to love listening when she, and Annie Lawlor in No.32, talked about the neighbours in colourful language as they cleaned each other's scalps with cotton wool balls and homemade eau de cologne; hair washing for the elderly being regarded as dicing with death.
'Lace curtains and no knickers' (ostentatious),
'Common as muck' (vulgar),
'Brass necked hoor', (no shame)
'A holy show', (letting yourself down, or if you were a child 'showing up' your parents),
'Eats high off the hog' (well nourished, no shortage of money),
'Reads the news offa the table' (too poor to have a table cloth)
'That skinny-malink wan' (bean pole)
'As round as a firkin'(as broad as she is long)
or a sigh and a lament and a
'God be with the days when you'd get change for a farthing'.
I never did discover what a 'hoors melt' was.

Picturesque turns of phrase were always remarkable. It was only after I lived in England for several years that I realised that we were Nations divided by a common language. English as we speak it in Ireland does not allow for a simple 'Yes', 'No' or other single word reply. We always answer in statement form, probably as a result of having to learn our catechisms off by heart!

A typical Dwellings exchange would be;

'Howeya Mary (shouted from one of the balconies to somebody passing by) 'Are youze keepin well?

'Yes, tanks be to God, Fit as a flea, and yer self?

'A bit shook up with an aul cough, but soldierin' on God willin'.

'And is yer Ma good'?

'Grand, dow dere'll be wigs on de green if I don't get home to take de clothes offa de line'.

'Ah won't youze come in and have a cup-a-tae in yer hand'?

'Another time when I not lookin to catch de wead'er.'

'Will youze pass by tomorra after Mass and we'll have a chinwag'

'Dat'll suit me down to the ground'

'Please God, let de wead'er hauld'

'As likely as wen the sky falls and we all catch larks'!

'True for youze, but God is good' and tomorra's an udder day.

'Are you sure I won't be puttin' youze out'?

'A Jazzis only the landlord can do dah'.

English equivalent;

'Hello Mary are you keeping well'

'Yes, and you'?

'Yes fine'

'How is your Mother'?

'Ok'

'We must make a time to catch up'

Yes, drop in any time'

Not a redundant word or supplementary comment involved and woe betide you if you took the invitation at face value!

Chapter 9

The Da

Peter Paul Redmond, Gran's oldest child, my father, was born on the Feast of St Peter and Paul in 1909. He was followed by Martin Joseph born two days too late in March 1912 to be named Joseph Martin, so he was baptised Martin Joseph in honour of Blessed Martin de Porres who was waiting in line for Canonization. Of eight children only Martin and two others survived, Sheila born 1921 and Therese Mary (Tess) 1925 both delivered by Mrs. Kavanagh from No.30.

He went to St. Lawrence O'Toole's School in Seville Place, had a short stint with the nearby Christian Brothers when the family moved into the Dwellings, transferring to the Strand Tech at fourteen when he showed no intellectual capabilities, and then served an apprenticeship in the print under the watchful eye of Uncle Joe. His spelling expertise saw him rise from machine man to compositor, and live long enough to see his craft being taken over by computers and machines not unlike combine harvesters. His lack of academic qualifications coloured his life, and his children's, and fostered his belief that if you were bright enough you would get a scholarship, and if you weren't there was no point wasting money paying on your education. The injustice of this attitude created a lifelong rift between us because when I sat and passed a Scholarship Exam with honours I discovered I was not entitled to use it because his earnings were above the proscribed rate. Instead of paying up he decided to fight the adjunction leaving my widowed grandmother to foot the fees.

He became a member of the Irish Transport and General Workers Union early in his working life, and was already a Branch Official by the time he married my mother Julia Loftus from Co. Galway. *Why* they married was a mystery to his parent's and to us, his children, because he was a reluctant husband and father. When I started compiling a family tree I fully expected to find myself present in utero at the wedding, but discovered it was another thirteen months before I appeared.

He was not the kind of father who lingered at the tea table or enjoyed the comfort of his own fireside. 'Wait until your Father comes home' type of threats from the Ma, seeking to give authority to her ire, were wasted on us since he never did more than lower his newspaper and purse his lips, or say with resignation, 'Don't annoy your Mother, tell her you're sorry'. The worst punishment he ever came up with was to stop my comics for a week, but I made his life such an absolute misery that he went out and bought them and never did it again.

By the time he had three young children he was a Committee Member of the Union so spent a great deal of time at Liberty Hall, formerly the Northumberland Hotel, then the Union Headquarters on the Quays. I remember well the smoke filled imposing foyer, the Ma and me sitting on the shiny wooden benches, and Seán and Bridie sharing the warmth of a vintage Harris pram, waiting for him to come out of some meeting or other. Gran used to say 'Julia, wouldn't it be better to wait at home in comfort instead of down there in the cold? However Julia probably had her reasons. My father's easy charm, love of camaraderie and eye for the ladies fed her insecurities, so being there to escort him home meant he went home, but also meant an uneasy evening listening to the radio, or clearing the table to let him work away on Union Ledgers. He occasionally came home the worst for wear having had a session in the Butt Bar or Kelly's Pub with some cronies'; however he was a maudlin drunk who just fell asleep in an armchair.

He was awoken late one evening by a howling cat out on the back wall and went down to put a halt to its romance forgetting that four stone steps lay between the backdoor and the yard. Mrs. Mc Auley, our downstairs neighbour, a quiet, refined widow, found him some time later and the ambulance alert woke the street when it came to take him to the Mater. She was discretion itself when recounting the story but quietly told the Ma 'Julia, if he hadn't been so well oiled he'd have perished from the cold'.

The following day, as we prepared to go up to the hospital to visit him we saw him lurching down the Street on crutches with a full length plaster cast on his leg. He had fractured a femur and should have been on the Orthopaedic Ward in traction. Being a great believer in letting nature take its course he had taken his own discharge and returned home to the bosom of his family.

After several weeks of him being off work and under her feet, the Ma, was showing no overt manifestations of joy. He, of course, kept up some Union activities having the treasurer's ledgers and dues delivered to the house. The Ma got so fed up trying to gain access to the dining table that we had to resort to using the kitchen table cum worktop for eating. The 'comrades' were not ones for visiting the sick, but a remarkable amount of clinking brown paper bags were delivered by their children. The advantage of the contents of these bags to my sister and I was substantial. 'Fu Man Chu', the Rag and Bone Man amply rewarded us with balloons, whistles, windmills and a much prized monkey on a stick in return for the porter and baby Powers bottles. The peal of his bell and his call for 'Rags, bottles and jam jars' brought us running to his hand cart.

The Da got up one day and decided to remove the cast without benefit of x-ray or a doctor's opinion. Needless to say his leg never gave him a moment's trouble apart from some initial difficulty with a stiff knee, reinforcing his belief that doctors were a waste of money. Local kids dubbed him Hopalong Cassidy for months. He soon reverted to regarding Trinity Hall as his place of residence so in exasperation the Ma abandoned the three of us there one day. This should have been a traumatic experience for us, but the steady supply of Cleeve's Toffees, Fizz bags and Liquorice pipes from passing delegates kept us happy while we waited to be taken home. In a post war era of sweet rationing we didn't question whether the source was kosher or not, we just enjoyed the novelty of being the centre of attention. Eventually we went home with me pushing the pram, trying to see over the hood, the Da steadfastly refusing to push it for fear anybody would see him. He would reluctantly put a guiding hand on the handle to steer it, but only when I was in the process of mowing somebody down. The Ma's drastic action seemed to bring my Da to his senses, but it wasn't till shortly before she died that Ma got the attentive husband she craved.

Chapter 10

Fading Glory

I have no idea whether or not my father applied for a tenancy at the Dwellings but my first short lived address was No.95 Harcourt Street, on the south side, allegedly haunted by a weeping woman. This may have precipitated the move back over the Liffey to the north side Upper Rutland Street where I spent my first birthday. This Street had a wide thoroughfare of symmetrical Georgian houses numbered from 1 to 49. The numbers started from the left hand side of the street, curving around the large Wesleyan Methodist Church facing down the street at the top, and the numbering continuing down the right hand side until No. 49 faced No 1. In the nineteen forties there were only three vintage street lamps which had remained unlit throughout the Emergency, so to go out at night was folly without a carbide bicycle lamp to light your way, but the gloom was atmospheric and of the original era of the houses.

Looking up the street from Summerhill some of the houses which had stood on the spot from the last decade of the 18th century had aged and decayed, while others had stood the test of time. They came in three broad categories, the gaping door tenements with a family to every room as in Buckingham Street and Summerhill, the houses with closed hall doors tenanted by floor, and lastly, owner occupiers living in genteel poverty and the faded grandeur and elegance of yesteryear. The latter took lodgers disguised as country cousins.

The open door of No.48 was different.

It was a sanctum for local men. It gave them a quiet private place free from interference or interruption from irritated wives and moithering children and provided succour from the cares of the world. Its impressive red and white pole identified its front room as our local Gentleman's Club. With its selection of reading material, unhurried service and the opportunity to philosophize to companions it was a male version of paradise. In an era when fathers took sons to have their hair cut there was seldom a reason for a woman to cross the threshold, so few did, expecting the same reception they would get if they entered a Saloon Bar. Joe Moran presided over this haven with clippers, razors and scissors and in return nodded sagely, widened the topics of conversation to circumvent dissent, or pampering a customer with hot towels and unctuous hair treatments. We never had to look at Granda's, the Da's or Uncle Christy's shorn locks to tell where they had been. The trailing smell of Joe's 'Murray's Pomade' was sufficient. This pomade provided shine and hold to the hair of men from all walks of life. It had a cloying musky smell and the thick consistency of Vaseline. Local men seldom washed their hair so Murray's was designed to hold the style for a long time. It was a bugger to wash out of pillow cases.

Our house, No.35, was on the corner of Summer Street which made a break in the terrace of houses giving us the advantage of a high side wall and a gate that provided an entrance for the bin men, the slop collection for Mrs. Duffy's pigs, fuel deliveries to our coal sheds, and access to our bike and pram shed. The back yard had a wide concrete path around a twenty foot square of tufty grass which was occasionally hacked back. Above the grassed area were four washing lines which made it useless as a play area and meant the women got their feet soaked if the grass was wet when they pegged out clothes. We lived in respectability in a second category house extravagantly renting the first floor, previously the drawing and sitting rooms of its ascendancy owners. We shared the house with a widowed Margaret Murray

(no relation of the pomade maker) and her two grown up daughters Kathleen and Rose who had the second floor and attic rooms. In what was previously the servant's quarters in the basement, Mrs. Mc Auley, also a widow, lived with her brother, Tom. For some reason the basement areas of the houses had no steps down to the basement entrances so Tom used the space to grow geraniums, lettuce, scallions and tomatoes in pots, and in a cat and slug free environment they did well. The Mc Auley's have the advantage of having their turf and coal delivered through the manhole cover in the pavement straight into their own coal hole.
Nelly O'Neill, a retired dresser from the Gaiety, and her friend Molly Keegan, an usherette from the same theatre, lived on the ground floor's former dining room and parlour and never, to my knowledge, kept anything behind their wallpaper!

While the house still had fine architectural features such as its original Georgian doorway and fanlight, corbels and a dado rail in the front hall, a grand mahogany staircase, ornate flute and flower pattern cornices and coving, and ceilings *of* ornate plasterwork crowned by rose moldings, it also had an air of damp and flaking decay and the primitive plumbing of a bygone era. The latter consisted of a communal outside lavatory and cold water tap. The only plumbing inside the house was a butler sink and another cold water tap on the half landing above our floor. This we shared with the Murray's. The landing was wide enough to draw a curtain across and have a wash down in private. The Ma was a great believer in hardy children, so cold water wash downs, drying our selves by the comfort of a coal fire were the norm, but not for her such rigours as she trailed up to the landing in her pink satin dressing gown, her kettle of steaming water and her sponge bag with Lily of the Valley soap and talc.

Our two rooms were on a grand scale with marble fireplaces in both rooms. The room to the rear had one large eight pane window which shuttered across for privacy but with nothing but a former stable block out the back we were not overlooked. The proportions of the room meant that it could be comfortably divided into a sitting and dining area at one end with a kitchen area to the right of the window and an ablution area to the left with an overhead Dutch airer, washstand containing basin and jug and a covered pail. This small area was hidden by a lacquered three panel screen. The bucket was for discarded water and night time peeing only and woe betide anybody who used it for anything more substantial. It was never too dark or too cold to use the outside loo. Being used to the more primitive arrangements of our country relations, we complied.

The front room, the whole width of the house, was the family bedroom.

The two double beds and cot made little or no inroads on the space and even with a substantial wardrobe, tall boy and chest of drawers there was room to play in the centre of the room. Cleared of furniture it had been used for Sheila's wedding reception, seating forty, leaving room to dance to the Ma's big band ninety eight rpm records long after the bride and groom had departed for their three day cycling honeymoon in Tralee. This room had two windows dressed with lace curtains. It also had wooden concertinaed shutters, which when closed kept in the heat. The fire was seldom lit, my mother's explanation being that Father Christmas wouldn't come down a dirty chimney. I believed her for a time because some children never had a visit from him.

I look back with affection on the occupants of No.35. Their kindness to us, and to my mother in her final months, was unstinted, and Nelly and Molly never saw us short of free tickets for Matinee's at the Gaiety. Our seats may have been up in the God's but we still found the shows magical. Their over mantle was full of framed signed photographs of theatrical glitterati, Milo O'Shea, Jimmy O'Dea and Maureen Potter taking pride of place.

No 36, was at the other corner of Summer Street so No.35 and No.36 were separated by the width of the street. They both had side entrances but little else in common. No 36 was an out and out tenement with a family to every room and an open hall door. While our house exuded quiet refinement No 36 had a house full of 'dealers' who anywhere else would be called hawkers. These were strong women, good grafters and the mainstays of their families.

It was a volatile house with constant fights, usually as a result of the women showing solidarity if one of their neighbour's husbands came home drunk with violence to his wife or children on his befuddled mind. He would be beaten out into the street with anything that came to hand. Although Fitzgibbon St. Garda Station was nearby nobody ever went running there for help, nor was it unusual for a passing Rozzer to turn a blind eye and a deaf ear to a miscreant's cough being softened. Telephones were nonexistent and I would be hard put to tell you where the nearest one was if anybody had the urge to dial 999 or that, in fact, such a system existed.

The dealers set off early every morning wheeling their prams down the middle of the street to pick up their particular wares. 'Hairy Mary' an entrepreneur if ever there was one, was a flower seller at Nelson Pillar during the week, a peanut seller outside the Zoo at weekends changing to 'favours and minerals' outside Croke Park on match days. On fine evenings she sold toffee apples outside No.36, a treat I was never allowed to buy, not because we couldn't afford it but because of my Ma's hygiene obsessions. Mary's apples were on a par with Bina's refreshments in Claregalway, strictly verboten, however I did manage the odd bite from a luckier playmate, Bernie Moran, who's Ma was less picky about germs.

During the freezing winter of 1947 there wasn't a flower to be had but Mary, ever enterprising, set up an oil drum in the back yard of No.36 and baked potatoes. The smell wafting across Summer Street was irresistible.

I cannot, with any certainty remember Hairy Mary's given name, but I think she was Mary Crowe. This is only based on a vague recollection and a rhyme we used to sing

'Ravin' Mary was a crow
Her beady eyes missed nuttin'
Her hairy face was a pure disgrace
And her haunch would make good mutton'

Looking back, after a lifetime of nursing, Mary probably had polycystic ovaries but as children we were uncaring little bowzies.

My father continued to live at 35 following the Ma's death, while we, his children moved to live with the Gran and Granda in the Dwellings. In the sixties the street was demolished in the inner city slum clearance. Like a lot of Georgian and Regency Dublin these streets around Summerhill have been consigned to the memory of the kids who were reared there.

Chapter 11

The Ma

Julia Loftus, my mother, was born in 1908. She was born down the bog road in Gortcloonmore which was two miles from the nearest village in Claregalway in Co. Galway. Her family moved to nearby Cloonbiggen when the Land Commission divided land sequestered from local Ascendency Landlords so her walk to school was shortened by a mile. The daughter of Mary Bridget Qualter and Thomas Loftus and one of five children, she found life as a farmer's daughter not to her liking, and knowing she would be dependent on a dowry to marry, she persuaded her parents to fund a Domestic Science Course in Dublin. They did so knowing she would be safe in the bosom of the Presentation Nun's with whom she was lodging and that her training would be as good as any dowry. Her only friends from home were Delia Lenihan, a cousin, four years older, who had come to Dublin to train as a nurse. This was a source of envy to the Ma whose parents would have been unable to afford the fees. It didn't help that Delia married well and lived in relative comfort in the middle class suburb of Dundrum. The Ma's other friend, Roddy Kelly, who had been born in America, could always cheered her up when he visited bringing news and small treats. Another friend, but not from Claregalway, was Beatrice Murphy's mother from Rutland Cottages, I think they had worked together when the Ma, Diploma acquired, worked in the silver service dining room of the Iveagh Hotel, moving up to the prestigious and exclusive Royal Dublin Golf Club. This should have been a hotbed of opportunity for a glamorous and good looking young woman to find a husband.

Granny Redmond used to say '*That woman* would have been much happier if she had married a man who could have given her a ladies maid and nursery nurse to be at her beck and call'. However, she married my father giving birth to four children in four years me, in 1938, Julia who died at birth in 1939, Bridie in 1941 and Seán in 1942 and lived a discontented life until her death five years later. She never felt easy consorting with the neighbours who were born and bred Dubliners, and seldom crossed the thresholds of the other families in the house. On warm evenings women would sit out on the front steps, watching their children playing, chewing over the gossip, and slandering anyone who wasn't there. The Ma never participated, and when Sheila used to defend her saying she wasn't bred to it, an irate Gran would snort

'It's nothing to do with her being bread and buttered here, *that woman* thinks she's too good for Upper Rutland Street'.

The Ma remained *that woman* until it became clear that her diseased mitral valve, a legacy of childhood rheumatic fever, was going to kill her, then Gran, forgiving her airs and graces took her on as a daughter and she became Julia, or much to our amazement '*your poor mother*'. However old habits die hard so there was still some teeth sucking and muttering from the Gran when irritated by the Ma's Domestic Science pretensions. 'Why, in God's name she has to call the feckin thing a casserole when it's a poxy stew is beyond me' Gran would mutter when her daughter in law insisted on describing Gran's scrag end of lamb stew as a casserole. Her response to the Ma's calling her braised chicken 'coq au vin' is so vulgar it should be left to the imagination.

Looking back on my eight years with Julia as my mother I have never felt really bereaved by her death, but when Granny Loftus had died two years before I had been grief stricken, and knew that somebody who had cared for me had disappeared from my life. I also knew that if Granda or Gran Redmond died it would feel like the end of the world had come, but the Ma's death just left feelings of regret and guilt. Her nurturing abilities were erratic to say the least. When she was happy she was great fun and would pull the Da to his feet to dance to her big band records or let my friends and I dress up in her clothes including her silver fox fur collar. We would meet the Da from Liberty Hall and go to Forte's Ice Cream Parlour in O'Connell Street and share a Knickerbocker Glory, or the Parthenon in Talbot Street for a boat of Italian Ice Cream covered in raspberry syrup with a fan shaped wafers stuck in the creamy vanilla scoops. Tea in Woolworth's in Henry Street with full waitress service was a winter treat although we inevitably finished with jelly and ice cream.

Occasionally on a Friday, if the Da was home for tea, I would be send to Staffieri's chipper on Summerhill for two 'one and ones' and 'two singles,' Italian chipper parlance for two fish and four portions of chips. Romeo was a fiery tempered little roly poly Italian from Cassalattico with a halo of dark hair. He constantly roared at his sister Maria, whom everybody called Mary. Locals often threatened to duff him up, but Mary would just smile and say *'Hea no meen it'*. Why did we go in there? Well Romeo was the best fish and chip fryer in Dublin, and Mary's portions were always generous. If North William Street School was anything to go by there was also probably enough local Italians to keep him in business. In my class alone we had at least a dozen with names ending in 'ella' or 'anna' from Carmella to Gulianna with a handful of Annunciata's, Assumpta's and Concepta's thrown in to broaden the choice.

On the Ma's introspective days we left her in peace to listen to her records or write letters home or to her Aunt Julia, her namesake, in Indiana, but on her 'For God's sake get out from under me feet days' we retreated to the streets, or the comfort of Nelly O'Neill's rooms because we knew that when the nagers were on her whatever we did would irritate her. These periods of irritation with everything and everybody were interspersed with parental rows, and just when you felt like moving down to Gran's everything would be back to normal for days, even weeks, but we always waited in anticipation for the next squall. So it is sad to say, that when she told us she was going to die, she was at last providing stability in our lives, and assuring our future by leaving us in the care of Gran and Granda.

I remember very little of my mother's condition as she faded from our lives and died peacefully at home on the 20th of April 1947, two weeks before I made my First Communion. Gran provided a last service for her by laying her out with the aid of Mrs. Mc Auley. There was talk at the time that she had chosen her own coffin. If this is the case she did herself proud and I'm sure Mr. Jennings was rubbing his hands in delight as his top of the range model was taken up the steps of No 35 to Wake her.

Although there wasn't a cut flower to be had because of the prolonged frosts Hairy Mary turned up with a pram full of daffodils on one of the wildest days of the year when south west gale force winds closed Collinstown and the North Wall, and a rain lashed Dublin had its streets washed. At her Vigil the evening before her funeral the walking pace hearse made the short journey down to the Tin Chapel followed on foot by the drenched neighbours with whom she has failed to mingle, and the families in the house who had been so good to her. She never regarded Our Lady of Lourdes as her Parish preferring the Jesuits in Upper Gardiner Street, never missing the Nine Day Novena of Grace to their founder, St. Francis Xavier. Too weak to attend it a month or so before her death it gave her some consolation to hear from Mrs. Mc Auley that the overflow of devotees had blocked the traffic in Gardiner St and around Merrion Square indicating that the church, side chapels, and hall, seating about a thousand, had been filled to capacity.

After her Funeral Mass the following morning the cortege left for the burial with a coffin covered in sheaves of daffodils, the provenance of which remained a mystery but the drifts in Fairview Park were notably sparse as we passed on our way to Glasnevin. At the graveside the daffodils came in to their own as they created a golden blanket of delight on a bleak newly filled in rectangle of clay.

Chapter 12

Mind Me Domes

Our move down to the Dwellings had taken place gradually over February and March of 1947 so we were well established in our new abode by the time of my mother's death. As a self centred eight year old I gave no thought to the total upheaval taking on three young children was going to have on this elderly couple's life. With their own children flown the nest, Gran and Granda were living in relative comfort at 31 Artisans' Dwellings. In the ethos of the time their neighbours would have said they were only doing their duty, but they never made us feel we were a 'duty'.

While we may have stretched their budget we were provided with a home rich in care and love, and we responded with the ingratitude of most children. I know that their influence formed us and defined our experiences in childhood, becoming, as they did, our role models. They instilled in us a belief in hard work and honesty, a sense of justice, to have respect for others but to have the courage of our own convictions. More importantly we were always expected to 'show a bit of gumption' as they would succinctly put it.

It was a terrible sin to have no gumption!

The Gran's pragmatic belief was waste not, want not, and letting nature take its course. Granda's philosophy was more revolutionary 'Live on your knees or die on your feet'. The latter was the road he chose when he joined the Workers Party as a young man, but the savagery of the Civil War put an end to all heroics and now, past his prime, he lived in a country of bigotry, cronyism and gombeen men, or as he put it; gombeen men, gobshites and cute hoors!

The biggest change in our lives was the size of the flat. Being used to rattling around in the faded grandeur of a draughty Georgian house, the Artisans' Dwellings flats were small. They consisted of a big square room which was a sitting cum dining room, a good size bedroom leading off it, with a window looking out on to a balcony, and an architectural feature I have never seen before or since, a door from the main room to a balcony kitchen cum scullery. This had a tiled floor, a Belfast sink and draining board, a small coal shed with a tin bath hanging on the wall and a door leading to a water closet at the far end. The outer wall of the balcony was about four foot high and like the stairwell windows was open to the elements. It was overlooked by the tenants on the top floors of the tenements opposite, so for added privacy, Gran had a row of geraniums and pots of herbs along the parapet, nurtured through the winter wrapped in newspaper. It was Granda's opinion that the 'Company' had approved this open air arrangement to reduce the local incidence of tuberculosis. I'm not sure whether it did, but it certainly ensured a living for local milliners since every mature woman cooking in their open air kitchens wore a hat. The younger ones opted for a turban, the latter often covering a head full of curlers or pipe cleaners. The flat itself was cosy with a range in the front room spreading its warmth through the wall of the bedroom. We all shared the same bedroom when we first moved in, Gran and Granda in the double bed, me, and Bridie, head to toe in a single bed with Seán aged five in a trundle bed across the bottom. One tallboy had been moved out to the front room leaving a second for the three of us and all our worldly goods. We each had a cardboard box for what few toys we had which were kept under the bed. Apart from a large camphor laden wardrobe that was the contents of our communal bedroom. I defy any modern child to get all their possessions into two drawers and a cardboard box. How larger families managed is beyond me but they all presented tidy and well ordered front rooms, while their sardine packed bedrooms remained their private concern.

Over time, and coinciding with me coming down with the whooping cough, not called the hundred night cough for nothing, my grandparents moved their bed into the front room sacrificing the space from their two armchairs, which were seldom used, Granda preferring his cushioned captains chair by the range with his feet on the fender and Gran seldom sitting on anything but a kitchen chair when she *did* sit down, which was seldom. She was as thin as a whippet and on the go from morning 'til night. Whooping cough or not I was sent to school every day well dosed with Buckley's 'It tastes awful, but it works' Cough Mixture from Wagner's Chemist, and the more soothing Hippowine and Squills at night to allow everybody to get some sleep. I had my fair share of other childhood diseases and I'm sure I was a veritable 'Thyroid Mary' to fellow pupils at North William Street School. How can I claim that? Well at prize giving on my last day at school I got a prize for being the only child who had never missed a day's schooling. Gran considered the prize should have been hers so gave my statue of St. Catherine Laboure pride of place on her little alter.

Gran had very few prized possessions but her collection of china and porcelain ranked high. Her 'delph' as she called it, was out of harm's way, out of our reach on the dresser, and shielded by the round dining table. On display on the bottom shelves was her willow pattern for everyday use, her Sunday and high days gold banded green art deco octagonal set on the top shelves, and packed away in the press underneath from the day of her wedding, her Worcester tea service. Wrapped in tissue paper, this set never saw the light of day except when it was taken out once a year to be gently washed in warm Lux suds. Granda used to joke that it had been on display during the Eucharistic Congress in 1932 in case the Papal Nuncio called in on his way to give the concluding Blessing of the masses in O'Connell Street.

The bane of our lives was her bloody 'domes'. Along the top of her old oak sideboard sitting on a long antimacassar were four glass domes containing Staffordshire regency figurines. Unfortunately the sideboard was in line with the front door so anybody putting on a coat or carelessly swinging a schoolbag over their shoulder was in danger of sweeping the lot to the floor. 'Mind me domes' was a dire warning as we came and went, and much to everybody's amazement they survived our childhood, hence the visiting grandchild who yanked on the antimacassar and swept them to their doom shall remain nameless. We all looked on in frozen horror at the carnage expecting the Gran to condemn the child to the fiery furnaces of hell, but she just replenished the teapot, shrugged, and said 'Well it had to happen sooner or later'.

Chapter 13

Awful times

Gran never had the dubious benefit of the Ma's Domestic Science training. She earned her reputation during 'The Emergency' and the subsequent post war rationing. Put anything in front of her and she could cook it. Put anything in front of us and we would eat it. Not for us the extravagance of a silver side of beef, a shoulder of lamb or a roast chicken. Those were for special occasions. Our treats were coddle or scrag end of lamb stew, or for Granda, the occasional Quinn's well seasoned pork chop. Our main meal of the week was Saturday tea when my father joined us for a big breakfast type fry up with all the trimmings.

Perhaps I should explain meal times in Dublin 1.

Breakfast - mostly porridge

Dinner – mid day – main meal of the day

Tea – small fry up or salad sandwiches – biscuits, or bread and jam if you were lucky.

Supper – leftovers – cup of cocoa

'Something in your hand' (there was no such thing as a snack).

In our house if you said you were hungry a carrot was proffered, or if it was cold out, a slice of bread covered in dripping or dunked in Oxo, or if we were lurking about when Gran was pickling beetroot, a slice of bread with hot slivers of beetroot sprinkled with sugar.

On a weekday morning, as soon as the ten o'clock Mass was over at St. Agatha's in Nth William Street, Gran would come home via Summerhill Parade and do her shopping on the way. Our daily fare was offal of every type and description and included sheep's head's, tripe, heart's, liver, ox tail, and calves feet, all scourged out of poor Mr. Butler one of the butchers on Summerhill. He would point to the prices painted in white wash on his shop window in vain. Mr. Quinn, the pork butcher was made of sterner stuff but even he used to succumb to her schmoozing, she claiming kinship to him via her mother. From him she bought black and white pudding, crubeens, and pig's cheek's which she used to roast. Having fleeced him on the offal she would then threaten to go along to his competitors Granby's, Hefner's or Stein's for her sausages telling him his were more expensive. It was pointless arguing with her that his were a better product so he'd throw in a couple of extra sausages to keep her quiet. The only thing we all refused to eat was kidneys. Our corny joke about offal was *It's awful but we like it*.

Fridays, being a fast day, she went along Parnell Street to 'Magzer' Ryan the dealer who sold fish from an old pram. Magzer had a voice well seasoned by smoking so she could out croak every dealer along the row. She had a slab of marble across the pram to use as a gutting table with the fish in melting ice in crates behind her, and surrounded by scabby cats. Despite a sign, misspelt, and saying '*Do not handle the gods*' Gran examined the eyes and scales of every mackerel or herring she bought. Gran must have been known to Magzer who called her 'Jools' and always threw in some roe without being asked. But even here the Gran couldn't resist bartering and Magzer would say in her corncrake voice 'Jazzis Jools, if you want it for that price you'll have to go out to Howth or catch it yourself', or when she was on the verge of giving in, 'Muddah a God Jools *lave* me some profit', I've got a houseful of chislers to feed', but Magzer knew that she would get more sympathy from Madame Defarge knitting by the guillotine than from 'Jools' Redmond in search of another farthing off her Friday fish.

Fruit and vegetable buying was a nightmare because although there were several such shops along Summerhill she would traipse me down to the vocal bedlam that was Moore Street Market on a Saturday morning to pick and choose from her favourite stalls. The cacophony of cries of get your 'apples an' noranges' here, 'best King Edwards and Savoy over here' ta'ma'is an' scallions and the makin's of a salad, one and six here' was deafening. Gran was well known by the dealers who never tried to bluff her with less than perfect specimens of their particular produce. I would be sulking like mad, and be laden with bags all the way home while Gran would make a detour for bread.

When it came to bread she constantly changed from Kennedy's, to Boland's, to Downe's and on to Johnson, Mooney and O'Brien. Distance was no object if she could save a couple of pence, or could time her visit to get bread from the day before which was half price, and before sliced bread, was known as 'cutting' bread because it was firmer and easier to cut than bread straight from the oven. Her first preference was Johnson, Mooney and O'Brien because they were Quakers, good to the poor, and their philanthropy non-denominational.

The only exception to her bargain hunting was milk.

Tierney's Dairy on Summerhill was cheaper than Tighe's, and Tierney's delivered, but Gran was convinced that the former watered down their milk. Added to that Tighe's Dairy was across the Street at No 10 and Gran approved of Mrs. Tighe's cleanliness, so she toddled across with her tin can early every morning to collect her milk, without quibbling about the extra ha'penny it cost. With the cows in a barn out the back in Bailey's Row you couldn't ask for fresher milk. The Gran also believed that Tighe's cows went back to the green fields of County Roscommon for their holidays.

Buying clothes with her was an even worse nightmare. I would rather have been dressed in schmutter from Cumberland Market than schlep the length and breathe of Talbot, Henry and George Street by her side. I'd have frock after frock fitted up against me in Boyer's, Cassidy's and Collette Modes with the Gran sucking her teeth or tut tutting. Having been a seamstress and a connoisseur of good cloth and finishes, she was extremely picky, so the warp and the weft were scrutinised, as were seams and the alignment of any pattern. I would have settled for a modified sack just to get her out of the shop. When we had driven the poor sales woman to distraction Gran and her would agree a selection for fitting on. This would raise the hopes of the sales woman that a sale was in the bag. I would be sick twirling, before a pronouncement of the magic words 'We'll take it', and then as I listened in horror, 'but not at that price'. 'Tell the Floor Walker I want to see her'. Floor Walkers were not women, or men, to be trifled with but, I had yet to find one who stood up to the Grans deprecation of their stock and shoddy finishes without caving in and giving her a discount. We would go home, she well pleased with her bargain, me sighing with relief, She would say, with satisfaction 'There's a good quality cotton in that frock, and we'll soon have the finish up to scratch' And she'd be as good as her word, Sunday morning I'd be wearing a custom finished frock with a hand turned hem and smart buttons from her collection.

One thing Gran cooked properly was cabbage. She cooked it only long enough to make it soft and with a knob of butter on it we shovelled it down. Aunt Sheila boiled the balls off hers and was always annoyed when we turned up our noses at it. With the Dwellings open air kitchens you could smell cabbage cooking on every balcony, but at least it didn't hover about unlike our front room which smelled of cooking all winter long because Gran kept a stockpot on the go on the range.

She supplied five or six families with stock, and bunches of thyme and parsley as a basis for their stews. When dried fruit and candied peel came off ration, and mixed spice was to be had again, she resumed making bread pudding which we loved, but not to the extent that we would swap it for a piece of shop bought gur cake from Lemass's. Homemade broken biscuit cake was another winter favourite. One of the Breslin's worked in Jacobs so was a reliable source of broken biscuits in return for Gran's broth. The cake didn't require cooking, but in an era before fridges, like jelly, it had to be put out on the window sill or balcony parapet to firm up. It would be covered with a plate, with a big stone on top, and like jelly, the gulls would smell it streets away and come swooping down to try to get at it. Our second line of defense was the Rag and Bone Man's multicoloured Bakelite windmill, but some of the seagulls were big as eagles and afraid of nothing. Their raucous screeches of defeat when thwarted would echo around the rooftops, but their successes were discrete, and often only discovered when somebody went to retrieve the family treat. I often wondered why we were not persecuted in the same way by pigeons. Had we eaten them all? Rice also became available again so rice pudding was back on the menu and on a cold winter's night, if we were lucky, we would have a bowl of goody. Other children would be pampered with this if they were ill, but illness wasn't encouraged in our house so we never associated it with comfort food because no doctor passed over our doormat throughout our childhood. For us, the philosophy was the survival of the fittest

Chapter 14

In sickness and in health

A visit from the Doctor cost money so families were dependent on free hospital clinics were they endured long queues and the ministrations of medical students. The Summerhill Dispensary, or the Welfare Clinic as it was known locally, provided services for Mothers and Children. It immunized children and treated infectious skin conditions, and was probably involved in ante natal care. In 1950, following the advent of the National Health Service in Great Britain there was a proposal to introduce a scheme in what was by then the Republic of Ireland which would provide free maternity care for all mothers and free healthcare for all children up to the age of sixteen, regardless of income. The Bill met with ferocious opposition from conservative elements in the Catholic hierarchy and the medical profession so most local women went through pregnancy without medical care, depending on family or a 'Bona Fide' midwife to deliver the baby at home. Bona Fides were woman who had been licensed to practice but who had not gone through a recognised training for certification. The only thing *we* used the Dispensary for was collecting our Cod Liver Oil and Malt.

Coming from a family who believed in letting nature take its course, an immunisation needle never penetrated our skin, nor were we ever painted with lurid Gentian Violet or Mercurochrome Red, which let the whole neighbourhood know who had ringworm, impetigo, scabies, or 'leather blisters' medically known as molloscum contagiosum. I know because I caught the latter from Beatrice Murphy despite her being the cleanest child in the neighbourhood.

To protect us from diphtheria and other throat infections we were taken to 'Adam and Eves' on Merchants Quay on the Feast of St. Blaise to have our throats blessed. It didn't work for Éamon who was incarcerated in the overflowing Cork Street Fever Hospital for Notifiable Diseases, with diphtheria. He survived, therefore renewing the family's faith in St. Blaise, Mother Nature, and the power of prayer, however a lot of children died from diphtheria or scarlatina, either through ignorance or because their parents couldn't bear to abandon them at the hospital door.

No bedside visiting was allowed so their despairing children lived or died in isolation. For those fortunate enough to recover an added cruelty was that parents and children were allowed to briefly view each other through a glass screen on Sundays curtailed after ten minutes so as not to upset the children!.

The less said about the folklore of the time and the beliefs of the Gran in the efficacy of goose fat rubbed on chests, and torsos rapped in brown paper the better. Suffice to say while I may have succumbed to the brown paper under my liberty bodice, goose fat was out. We also survived vapour rubs, mustard and bread poultices, onions tied to feet at bedtime to draw a cold and the occasional hot toddy to keep us quiet!

Saturday mornings was also hair washing morning and we were not allowed out until it was dry (the reason for this also belongs in folklore). I was the only one with long hair so I had to black lead the range or red raddle the balcony floor while waiting for it to dry, and it was time for Gran to put on her coat and take me out shopping with her. I used to speculate how many years off purgatory I would get for every time I had to accompany her.

'None', Bridie Fitz used to tell me, with conviction, 'You don't offer it up to God' (i.e. suffer in silence),' you whinge about it, so it doesn't count.' I didn't know then about the Prodigal Son option.

Chapter 15

The Nun's

North William Street School aka Naomh UinSeánn Scoil Náisiúnta ó Cailini, run by the Daughters of Charity of St Vincent de Paul took us through their door age four, and spat us out again ten years later, the girls that is, the Bhuachaille went off to the Christian Brothers at about the age of eight. For a lot of children this was their only education because compulsory education ended at fourteen and it was legal to start work. There was no such thing as a 'teenager'; you were either a school child or a young working adult. The Nuns had to set us up with enough skills and knowledge to start out on the road of life, or to get us through a scholarship to continue our education if our parents couldn't afford it, and were willing to defer the prospect of a wage packet coming into the home. You either loved school or you hated it, I loved it. I had attended 'William St' when we lived in Upper Rutland St. so continued to do so when we moved to 'the Buildings' despite Rutland St. School being on our doorstep.

Going to the Nuns meant we had to cross Portland Row, a wide thoroughfare that was part of the North Circular Road, which lead down to the North Wall and the cattle boats for England. On cattle market days coming home from school we would have to stand out of harm's way and watch the massive cattle drive coming from the market further up the North Circular.
When the cattle pens were opened cattle stampeded down the long straight road to the boats. They were driven by fit young men with long sticks running alongside. You would hear the thunder of hooves in the distance before hearing the shouts of

the drovers. The cattle came into view as they crossed Summerhill then they came down the hill past the 'Old Maids' Home in a cloud of dust, The drovers were not shouting at the cattle but at kids taking their lives in their hands daring each other to run across the road before the cattle reached them. I could feel my brother's hand twitching with excitement in mine dying to make the run. I told him I would kill him before the steers even reached him, which put a halt to his suicidal intent, but once he moved further up the North Circular to the Brothers at Candice's he was out of my jurisdiction. However he lived into his sixties so he must have learned some sense

Both of my aunts, Sheila and Tess, had attended North William Street so there was never any talk about us going anywhere else. I remember very little of my first three years apart from being given a shiny new penny on my first day and being awestruck by the huge white seagull type headgear the Sister's wore with their long woven blue habits. In an era where the prevalent philosophy on children's behaviour was 'speak when you're spoken to, come when you're called, close the door after you and do what you're told' I learned to stand silently in line at the end of play time, to sit with my arms folded when instructed to do so, not to run on the stairs, and to curtsy to Sr. Monica, the Headmistress before speaking to her. The only rule I didn't keep was 'children should speak only when spoken to'

Like a lot of Irish Mammies, the Ma, used certain adjectives before the names of her children. Seán was 'my Seán', Bridie was 'poor Bridie' primarily because I used to bully her, and I was 'that Bernadette Mary' because I would argue with the Devil. The infant classes were taught by lay teachers who were obviously of the same mind as the Ma, so when Bernie became Bernadette Mary I knew I was due for a visit to Sr. Monica's Office 'for acting the maggot'. The outcome was not punishment as anticipated, Sr. Monica, in her wisdom, decided to put me up a class which solved the problem, until the incident of the Prodigal Son several years later.

In my First Communion year I went into Sr. Francis' class. The Jesuits allegedly said 'give me a child until the age of seven and I will give you the man'; well, with a change of gender and substituting 'at' for 'until' I believe the same could be said for 'Sr. Francis' girls. The system at the time was you had the same teacher for the next five years, so if you were unlucky enough to get one who made you miserable, as did Bridie, and my cousin Carol, you were stuffed. Your only hope was to get a parent to go up to the school and ask to have you transferred to the other class for your particular year. Few parents did so believing that it must be your fault for not working hard enough, or for annoying the Nun in the first place. Nobody ever questioned whether they were rotten teachers or even had a Teaching Diploma. Sr. Francis, with or without a Diploma, was a born teacher and over the next five years I learned never to let a day go by without looking up a word I didn't understand, to pace my way to school memorizing the spelling of ten words, or a times table we'd been set. History and geography she taught as one subject so having had a history lesson on 'The Sieges of Limerick' we would then open our geography books, look at the lie of the land, the influence of the Shannon, materials for reinforcing the barricades and discuss factors that enabled Patrick Sarsfield to blow up the artillery wagons. She was a devotee of Frank Bunker Gilbreth a time-and-motion-study father who taught his twelve children (Cheaper by the Dozen) never to do one task when they could be doing two. I'm sure Sr. Rita, who taught in the boys school would have heartily disagreed with her.

The Nuns were realists knowing that most of the knowledge we were acquiring was not going to put a crust on the table so we also learned how to knit, sew, embroider, darn, crochet, make a button hole, turn a collar, and hand wash clothes. We each had a display book with examples of our sewing and knitting expertise. The 'craft' book contained cardboard pages to which we tacked on a knitted square with a darn in it, one glove, one sock, an embroidered handkerchief with an invisible hem, a circle of crochet work, and a doubled over piece of cloth with a button and button hole. Despite being left handed my sewing was very neat and my knitting had tension to die for, so Sr. Francis entered my work at some kind of Exhibition at the Mansion House. I was given a 'Highly Commended' certificate by Andrew Clarkin, the Lord Mayor of Dublin. This cut no ice with Granda who regarded him as one of De Valera's 'hoors', a man who was too lazy to wind his own clock, the clock in question hanging from his coal merchants shop in Pearse S. and being a source of derision at the time by Flann O'Brian in his Miles na gCopaleen column in the Irish Times. Gran was delighted, and saw me following in her footsteps as a seamstress but I had to disillusion her. While I may have been skilled at these crafts they bored me to death, so there was no way in hell I was going to earn a living from them. 'Poor' Bridie was useless at knitting, and her sewing was always bloodstained, so the Gran waited in vain for a matching sock and glove.

In years to come, in a busy Casualty Dept my stitching expertise stood me in good stead sewing up drunks who neither knew nor appreciated Sr. Francis' legacy, but many a ham fisted House Officer and medical student did, as I stood over them teaching them the art, with a lot less patience than Sr. Francis when she stood over us, and many a poor old soul on the

Geriatric ward appreciated Sr. Agnes' junket, or in the early hours, a bowl of the Grans 'goody'.

In our 'domestic science' class Sr. Francis took us over to the convent kitchen and with the aid of Sr. Agnes taught us how to clean our hands properly with a nail brush, how to sort clothes for washing (something I wished I'd remembered the first time I loaded a washing machine), the art of making proper cucumber sandwiches (a skill I would require some ten years hence), how to knead soda bread, and make batter for drop scones.

We took our cooking efforts home for the Gran to praise and poor long suffering Granda to eat. I also learned how to make junket, caramel custard and posset, how to set a table for a five course dinner and how to hold a knife and fork. I have gone through life watching, in amusement, others mishandling the latter and smile in remembrance of Sr. Agnes' telling us 'Girls, they are *not* knitting needles so don't hold them as such'. We also learned not to call napkins, serviettes.

1947 saw great excitement in North William Street School. One of the nineteenth Century's Sisters of Charity, Catherine Laboure, was up for canonisation so we had to direct our prayers towards this goal. We were all given a Miraculous Medal to wear, and promised to include her in our prayers during the summer holidays and in return we would have a party in the autumn term.

We learned quite a bit about the Order leading up to the canonisation including the fact that our Nuns weren't Nuns at all. Our lot only took a simple personal vow yearly, not a perpetual vow like proper nuns, so they didn't *have* to dedicate their lives to us. Those of us in Sr. Francis' class speculated about whether she would get fed up and leave us, while Bridie, in St. Madeline's class and, in time, Carol, who had Sr. Joseph prayed that their nuns wouldn't be able to resist the temptation.

There were three of us in my class with sisters in Sr. Madeline's class, who, in her eyes should be doing better, so she would send up a little note to Sr. Francis asking us to come and see her. We would go to her classroom and be castigated for not helping them with their homework. To plead that we had more than enough homework of our own was never going to get us into heaven *'if we were selfish enough not to give those less endowed a helping hand'* a sorrowful Sr. Madeline would murmur. This presupposed the fact that we were brighter than our sibling's, and that they had a burning desire to sit down and do their homework, but we knew that they were just bone idle little feckers who would rather be out playing. 'Showing us up' in front of Sr. Madeline never engendered sisterly love, so we would puck them all the way home, and threaten them with all kinds of torture if Sr. Madeline called us down again. It was actually Sr. Francis who saved their mangy little hides, at least from us, she just told her Sister in Christ to stop sending for us. However, having made us commit sins of blasphemy, and against charity, they were still responsible for stains on our immortal souls.

Not to mention Pugin's Venetian-Gothic style Orphanage attached to the school and convent would be remiss of me, but if truth be told, apart from envying them their lovely uniform, we knew little about the children there who were scattered thought-out our classes. They were known as 'Boarders' and wore 'Columbia blue' dresses with peach coloured collars in summer, and navy skirts and 'Royal blue' jumpers over snow white blouses in winter, while we had 'Navy blue' serge gymslips over a multitude of tops. Looking back they probably hated their uniform because it identified them as 'orphans' although few of them were. They also probably hated the 'invite an Orphan to tea' campaigns, but Moira Boyle who came to tea at Grans always seemed to enjoy it, however I think what she enjoyed most was running wild in the streets like the rest of us, because their everyday playground was the Convent grounds.

Chapter 16

A Penny for the Black Babies

Over the past few decades we have been appalled by stories of cruelty and abuse perpetrated in our Industrial Schools and Orphanages, but as children in the forties and fifties we were oblivious to it, as were most of our parents who were brought up to respect people in Holy Orders.

Altruism to those less fortunate than us was instilled in our guilty little souls as we remembered the Famine years and thanked God for our food, the clothes on our back, our health and strength and the grace of being born a catholic. Black babies had none of these things so a visit by the Society for the Propagation of the Faith showing films of deprived black babies, and our far flung Missionaries toiling in their midst always inspired us to take a Rosary Card in the hope of filling it in to get to name a Black Baby. The way this was achieved was to collect a ha'penny for every bead of the rosary, pricking a hole in each bead as you collected until you had florin. Then you wrote the Baptismal name you were giving your baby on the back. Family and neighbours were scourged until your goal was accomplished. William Street would no sooner have its quota collected when Rutland St. would have its Propagation visit. As well as this yearly collection we were expected to donate a penny a week to feed our babies, so I would be racked with guilt thinking of Patrick, Philomena, Catherine and Assumpta starving to death if I spent it on sweets instead.

The soulful beseeching eyes of the black babies on the Propagation poster outside Sr. Monica's Office haunted us, as they do to this day, on well known charity posters and TV appeals.

Father Damian's Lepers out in Surinam also had a claim on our compassion. I acquired enough knowledge of Leprosy from watching our yearly viewing of 'The Leper Priest' to be able to diagnose it in a Lascar cook from a merchant ship who came into a London Casualty Department with a burned hand. The loss of feeling in both hands and silvery patches on his trunk confirmed it for me, but I was only a student nurse so a scathing Registrar sent off skin samples to prove me wrong. Sr. Francis would have been proud of me, I knew my Hansen's disease when I saw it and probably knew more about it than he did being a proddie *and* educated in the echelons of an English public school. I probably knew a lot more about black babies too.

To ensure that we had no respite from unfortunates we also had our annual viewing of films on St. Vincent de Paul and St.Louise de Marillac the Founders of the Vincentian Missioners and Daughters of Charity. These films were to soften up our consciences before the yearly Mission. 'John Charles' thought that we didn't get enough fire and brimstone from our Parish clergy and he was probably right. As Monsignor O'Reilly got older and deafer his sermons became milder, and in a time before microphones were common in churches, inaudible, and his belief in a loving God shone through. Fr. Nix was new and unknown but Fr. Newth's intellectual sermons made you wonder if there was a God at all. Fr. Burke, who looked like Orson Welles, and could belt out hymns like Mario Lanza was relegated to frightening us children at the ten o'clock Mass on Sundays. Mick (as we irreverently called him) used to roar at us for about five minutes, mostly telling us to be good for our mammies, not to curse or to 'mitch' and to say our prayers and go to confession. We never took much notice of him but just in case he roared at me I always went to confession to Fr. Newth because he wasn't into castigation. He would just ask you quietly if you were *truly* sorry for your sins and then give you three Hail Marys. His absolution always sounded so sincere that you felt the least you could do was to put a bit of fervour into your penance and nor gabble it off on the run. At that time there was no such thing as getting out of going to Mass on the Sabbath, no copping out with a Mass on Saturday evening, so a lot of adults packed the back of the church at the children's Mass because of the short sermon and to listen to us singing. I quite missed Fr Burke when I joined the choir in 1948 because then I attended the twelve o'clock High Mass. By the time of Granda's funeral in April 1949 I was able to sing a Latin Mass. However his funeral service was held in Our Lady of Lourdes and was a melancholy affair

Chapter 17
The Men in Black

When the soutaned Redemptorists in their tricornered hats. and the black cowled Vincentian Missioners in long woolen habits, sandaled feet, and wooden beads hanging from a leather belt, came striding into town they struck trepidation into the hearts of saints and sinners alike, because unlike the Ku Klux Klan, this lot were after everybody. They may not have ridden in on horses or with burning crosses but the zeal burning in their eyes, and the smell of fire and brimstone in their nostrils made them as militant as their friends in white. Unlike Parish clergy the Missioners were the real Soldiers of Christ. For those of us children living in 'the Dwellings', Our Lady of Lourdes was our geographical Parish, but going to North William St. school put us in St Agatha's Parish, so our bodies, and souls, were claimed by both the Lourdes visiting soutaned Redemptorists and St. Agatha's Vincentian's for their Mission Week

When the latter was on we were excused homework for the week, but for Lourdes we had to do our homework before flocking to the Tin Chapel of an evening to listen to the ferocious Reds. The entertainment value and drama was great. Reluctant husbands were coaxed, coerced, and manhandled down Bella Street to join the rest of the neighbourhood to have 'the hard word' put on them, and sing 'Faith of Our Father's' with varying degrees of fervour. The 'craw thumpers' needed no inducement, filling the front rows with alacrity. Granda, a man of moderate habits, came to placate Gran, and not because he had any great need to, and would sit at the back with other grumpy old men passing out their Milroy's 'Cough No More' sweets and

Fisherman Friend lozenges to divert attention from the sounds emanating from their nicotine damaged lungs.

The dealers would have their prams and stalls set up with religious objects outside the church door. Scapulars, medal's, candles, encased relics, Holy Pictures and statues of Saints of every nationality were displayed. On the last night the Missioners blessed all these purchases and then we would all light our candles and renew our Baptismal vows. Any mother would tell you that to give a lighted candle to a child was folly, to give one each to dozens of children could be regarded as depraved indifference, but who was going to arrest a Soldier of Christ?

However a lot of the piety and good intentions were lost in the muttered curses of mothers separating children trying to set fire to themselves or others, so they were back to the Parish Clergy the following week with the same sins. Irene Fitzpatrick who'd had her good coat scorched was heard to say, on her way back home

'Jesus was only scourged once, but if he have to put up with my feckin lot then he'd know wha' being scourged every day of the week felt like'.

'May God forgive yiz Irene Fitz' Lena Breslin said, 'The poor Man died for your sins'

'There ya go' said Irene 'didn't give his feckin' mother a thought, did he'?

'Yizz"ll go to hell in a handcart' said a shocked Lena.

'Well, at least I'll be able to take the weight ofa me feckin corns on the way dere' retorted an unrepentant Irene.

The men who were 'fond of the gargle' were helpfully pointed out by Holy Joe's to the members of the Total Abstinence Society who were there on a recruitment campaign. With a splash of Holy Water from the font in the front porch the reprobates blessing themselves before making their way through the campaigners as they crossed the road to the solace of the Saloon Bar of the Gloucester Diamond, inviting the campaigners to perform anatomical feats I didn't understand as they did so.

A church forecourt full of bikes was a temptation to local bowzies who went Sundance Kid style riding around the streets while their owners were seeing to their immortal souls. However to give them their due the bikes were back on the forecourt before the church emptied, the little chislers who had promised to look after them, with their hand out for their expected minders fee. Stealing a bike then would be like stealing a car these days, and to acquire a bike was such a substantial expenditure that a thief would be as noticeable a Belicia Beacon. Bells and pumps were another matter.

Chapter 18

Cootes and Herons

While Sr. Francis had us for most of the day, we had Sr. Monica for Religious Knowledge and Poetry, and in time, she prepared us for confirmation. Sr. Monica had a lovely speaking voice, we suspected a British influence. She had a great interest in elocution, which wasn't on the Department of Education's curriculum but that didn't stop her. 'You may come from Summerhill she used to say, but by the time you leave North William St. you will sound as if you were born in Foxrock. None of us knew or cared where Foxrock was, but knew it was somewhere we should aspire to live. We soon learned what was expected of us as we had our gurrier accents metaphorically knocked out of us. We knew *never* to let a youze or a yiz past our lips. '*You*' was used for singular and plural, but luckily for me, who spent two months a year in the bogs of Galway, a plural '*ye*' was acceptable. At home we spoke with reasonable enunciation and articulation, despite being surrounded by dis, dat, dese and dose, a sparsity of Th's and only a nodding acquaintance with ing's.

It was only in the streets we used the Dublin vernacular because kids who went to Rutland Street School used to take the piss out of us if we didn't. You never had to ask a girl which school she went to, you could tell as soon as she opened her gob if she had been through Sr. Monica's hands, and if she were able to recite Alfred,
Lord Tennyson's 'The Brook', all thirteen sodding verses, it confirmed it. This poem was used to combine our Poetry lesson and our elocution session as we sat at our desks waiting for Sr. Monica's pointer, which was used like a baton, to point to each of

us at random to stand up and recite the next verse in clear BBC English. Go on try it. Articulate and annunciate every word;

I come from haunts of coot and her'n;
I make a sudden sally
and sparkle out among the fern,
to bicker down a valley.
By thirty hills I hurry down,
or slip between the ridges,
by twenty thorpes, a little town,
and half a hundred bridges.
Till last by Philip's farm I flow
to join the brimming river,
for men may come and men may go,
but I go on forever …

A year of that and you too could sound as if you came from Foxrock. To give Sr. Monica her due she instilled a love of poetry in most of us despite starting each lesson with her elocution practice, and knowing that we could speak 'properly' when required, did give us enormous confidence when we went into the world of work.

It was harder to tell which school a boy went to because they all used the vernacular in the street. Was it the Rutland Street Slaughterers or the Sado Brothers? In their case it all came down to grammar. They went to the Brothers if they knew the difference between 'who' and whom' and when to use 'me' and 'I'. Being predominately culchies the Christian Brother's may not have gone in for elocution, but they certainly taught my brother how to construct a grammatical sentence. There were also some fine teachers in Rutland Street but they had a daily battle with big classes, lack of funding and parents who didn't appreciate the value of a good education.

My big disagreement with Sr. Monica came about in our Religious Knowledge lessons. Bernie Moran who shared my desk, used to turn her pleading eyes on me and whisper 'Will you for feck sake shut up and not annoy her, or we'll both get the cane'. But I was unstoppable. We were now well into the Parables and had reached the Prodigal Son. This git had taken his inheritance and squandered it, then came back to tell his Daddy that he was sorry and his Da killed the fatted calf and forgave him, making his goody-goody shmuck of a brother mad as hell. Ergo, God was well pleased when sinners returned to the fold, so why be good, when you could be bad and be forgiven? Sr. Monica tried to argue that it was no skin off Goody Goody's nose because he still had his inheritance, but I wasn't buying it, sinners had all the fun. I think that was the thin edge of the wedge, a sceptic was born. I'd never have got through Confirmation without her judicious use of emotional blackmail.

In time to come in preparing for Confirmation we has to learn the hymn 'Faith of our Fathers' in which we declared that we were prepared to endure dungeon, fire and sword in defense of our faith, dying for it if necessary. I felt that God was asking just a bit too much but after the Prodigal Son incident Sr. Monica wasn't about to get into another theological discussion with a bolshi twelve year old. I could hear Bernie Moran moaning softly beside me.

'Tell me Bernadette Mary Redmond (my God!), has your Granny bought your Confirmation dress yet' Sr. Monica asked quietly without a hint of ire and with hands tucked into her muff like wide sleeves.

'Yes Sister', said I.

'Well now, I suggest that you go home and tell *her* you don't want to make your Confirmation'
Yeh, right 'I'd like me job', (or as today's kids would say, 'As if'
That was one sure way of dying for my faith.
As I knelt before Archbishop John Charles Mc Quaid the following week he touched my shoulder and murmured something in Latin over me, and I became cannon fodder in God's Army. As was customary I adopted a Saints name by added the name Térèse to my other two, thus securing an additional patron saint as protector and guide. I waited in vain for somebody to get mad enough at me to use all three. Nobody did but Bernie Moran moved desks anyway.

Chapter 19
Deck the Halls

Christmas in the Dwellings started on the Friday afternoon before Christmas when the schools broke up, and depending on which day Christmas Eve fell could mean days of persecution for every parent in the block. I was old enough to know that Santa Clause didn't exist, but Seán was still a fervent believer, and was afraid Santa would be too tired, to climb the stairs. Unlike our house in Upper Rutland Street which had a clean wide chimney, every flat in the Dwellings, had a chimney, but the chimney's ended in stove pipes attached to a range. This posed quite a problem for a man who ate high off the hog. Santa's solution was to visit while we were all at Midnight Mass, or he would knock on the door, leaving the presents in a pillowslip, and vanish before we could open it. Both of these solutions depended on the good will of a neighbour. Annie Lawlor usually did our landing being a believer that *'going out on the streets after dark was injurious to one's health*, so midnight mass was not on her agenda. All she would have had to worry about in those days was catching her death of cold.

The local entrepreneurs from about the age of eight upwards were out from dawn till dusk Christmas week foraging in leafier suburbs for holly and ivy, mistletoe and pine cones, fallen branches to be turned into kindling, stealing coal from the Phoenix Park, or collecting old peoples double ration of turf from the 27 Steps. They would also offer to wash down the landings, stairs and ground floor lobby for the women whose turn it was, and Christmas week that was often a godsend to mothers with a hundred and one other things to do. The money they made ensured that Santa called at their door even though the contents of the pillowslip were self financed. Very few families bothered with Christmas Trees. The flats were too small, so the wear and tear on parental nerves, and the resultant murdering of children and babies, who constantly knocked into them or pulled them over, was averted by not putting one up. However we did have decorations. Gaudy crepe paper ones, bought in Woolworth's, that concertinaed out into fantastic balls or bells, and were pinned on the ceiling at intervals among the criss cross of multicoloured bands of paper, we had individually licked to form chains. I'm sure licking glue on dozens of one inch by six inch pieces of coloured paper can't have been good for us; it used to take hours to get the taste out of your mouth.

Some floors decked the landings in holly to make up for the lack of a Christmas tree, or bought an evergreen wreath from the entrepreneurs for their front door, you then had to watch out that the little swine's didn't come back and swipe it to sell on to somebody else. With a certain amount of foresight Gran used to make her Christmas puddings before school broke up. She make enough to feed the five thousand so no family in our block of neighbours ever went without tasting a slice of pudding on Christmas Day, even the 'brass necked hoor' and the 'holy show'. She left her Christmas cake until Christmas was nearly upon us, so we always had the opportunity of licking out the bowl. I don't know why the poor woman ever bothered because Annie Lawlor and I were the only people who ate it. Granda didn't like marzipan, Bridie didn't like candied peel, Seán wouldn't eat squashed flies, my cousin Eamón only ate the icing and Gran usually only picked at Granda's discarded marzipan.

Christmas dinner arrived by milk train at Kingsbridge Station sent on its journey by Aunt May, my mother's sister, who had had Uncle Mick or her son Marteen give it into the care of the train Guard at Oranmore in Co Galway. Gran would take one of the young entrepreneurs with her to pick up the labelled brown paper parcel, 'a little Christmas box' would be passed discreetly to the Guard, and Gran and the urchin would bring home the eighteen pound goose.

In return for her Christmas dinner, the goose down and some goose fat, old Annie Lawlor would pluck the decomposing fowl and hang it in her balcony coal hole out of harm's way. Christmas dinner was always memorable. The frugal and penny pinching Gran would spend her rainy day money and enjoy it, but that's not to say that she spent money with gay abandon. One Christmas I was sure I was in line for a new coat, but when we set out for midnight mass there was my brown and yellow herringbone tweed coat, cleaned and pressed, and courtesy of May Grant's tailoring skills, with a two inch band of brown velour on the cuffs and hem, to give me some more wear out of it.

Midnight Mass in Our Lady of Lourdes little tin chapel was always well attended, the smell of porter from the back rows was overpowering. Most kids only went for the carol service before the Mass, and to see the baby Jesus being put in the crib, and then we were all off back home across the Bunkey Hill whose day time bombsite appearance was cloaked in a sparkly frost, and under a starlet sky could well have passed muster as the road to Bethlehem. The little ones rushing home to see if Santa has been, the unbelievers wondering if their Ma and Da had fulfilled their part in providing our hearts desire. Our Da, to give him due, and with the Gran in his ear, usually came up to scratch. The Gran filled our stocking with a cornucopia of small delights, nuts, a bar of rose or lavender smelling toilet soap, coloured pencils, a tube of rolos or smarties, new socks or mittens and down in the toe, an apple, or an orange when they were imported again after the war.

Being a woman with a lot of Christmas's under her belt she now left the nutcracker hanging out of my stocking in case we woke before her and started devouring the edible items in the stockings. The year before I had tried to crack a hazelnut with my teeth and a piece of it got stuck between two molars and had pierced my gum. There was blood everywhere, or so it seemed. Not wanting to darken the doorstep of Temple Street or the Dental Hospital Granda tried to get the piece of nut out with his cobbler's tweezers. My screams rent the air until it seemed that half Buildings were in the flat. Annie Lawlor proffered oil of cloves to dull the pain, May Grant advised a hot bread poultice to the side of my face, and Jim Fitzpatrick, in a new pyjama top and Sunday trousers, advised a good swill of whiskey to loosen the nut. I must have lost the will to live after that because the next thing I remember was Mrs. Bradley, the midwife from the Terrace, poking about in my mouth with something sharp, and the instant relief when she managed to retrieve the sliver of nut. Mrs. Bradley was a woman of great mystery who brought babies in her commodious carpet bag causing great commotion and screeching in the chosen household.

Throughout all of this chaos Gran had managed to get the goose stuffed, into the range oven, and, with all the trimmings, ready to eat on time. Granda and Jim Fitz, still in his pyjama top, were out on the landing debating the merits of whiskey as a local anaesthetic, while emptying a gill of Powers between them. Jim's new pyjamas were the source of much ribaldry and speculation, most men going to bed in their long johns. Pyjamas, if possessed, were kept for honeymoons or hospitals.

'I wonder how long it will be before they're over in Uncle's' said Annie to Gran busy setting the table.

'I wouldn't even give it till the New Year' said the Gran shrewdly.

Chapter 20

Credo in Unum Deum

Late in 1947 the organ at St. Agatha's was moved from a side chapel to a recently constructed gallery, so a choir was needed to accompany the newly refurbished organ, and fill the gallery. Sr. Kevin, from the boy's school was in charge of the choir and was looking for recruits. I thought I'd escaped because she only wanted those aged twelve and upwards, but my Aunt Sheila, a good friend of hers mentioned that I 'had a nice little voice' which only meant I could carry a tune, so before I knew it I was auditioned and recruited. Sr. Monica's elocution came in handy now because I had to learn a Latin Mass and Benediction service phonetically. By Easter 1948 I was ready to sing a Latin Mass. Today, sixty years on when the solo voice sings 'Credo in Unum Deum' I can still respond with a 'P-a-trem omni-po-tentem, factorem caeli et ter-rae, and sing the whole of the Creed. Even now I could sing a Latin Mass although there's not much call for it, the vernacular being used since the second Vatican Council.

There were advantages and disadvantages to being in the choir; the advantages being that you got out of lessons for practice, or a weekday Requiem Mass, the disadvantages were that you had to get up at the crack of dawn for the First Fridays Novena. That was the only time Annie Lawlor and the Gran went out before the streets were aired, believing that God would see them right, because the Graces accumulated for getting out of your bed on a cold and frosty morning to do the Novena, far outweighed worries about 'catching your death'. The church used to be well filled, so I always felt quite virtuous for making the effort.

The other disadvantage to being in the choir was that Sr. Kevin would want you to hang around after the Sunday Mass to discuss the finer points of descant, when you were rushing home to shovel some dinner into you before you made your way to the Strand or Lec queues for your afternoons entertainment.

Flash Gordon would wait for no man, or nun, for that matter.

Sheila and Christy had given Granda and Gran a gramophone for their fortieth wedding anniversary. Gran loved John Mc Cormack and the music of Stephen Foster, but Granda was an Enrico Caruso man. 'Ninety eights' were too expensive to buy, so he used to take a mooch down 'The Hill' (Cumberland Street Market) to look for second hand records. Taking Grans magnifying glass with him to examine them for scratches he acquired a nice little collection, my favourite being Ernest Lough singing Mendelssohn's 'Hear my Prayer'. We nearly wore it out playing it. Whenever I hear a boy soprano singing 'O for the Wings, the wings of a dove 'it transports me back in time to Granda and his wind up gramophone. The Christmas before he died he took me to a performance of Handel's Messiah at the Mercer's Hall. I'd much rather have gone to the pantomime at the Royal, but the experience and the music stuck with me a lot longer than subsequent pantomimes.

So, between Gregorian chant, Granda's records and the BBC Home Service, my musical education must seem strange, but in the late 1940's there was no 'top of the pops' and very few juke boxes. The only 'popular' music we heard was on the Light programme, or in Hollywood musicals, and very few of the latter, since the Strand or Lec picture houses catered for the cowboys and Indians brigade. The programme changed twice a week and comprised of a folly-in-upper, a 'B film', and then the main attraction in which the hero on horseback was always identifiable by his white Stetson. Cinemas were our main source of weekend enjoyment in the winter months. While some of them, like the 'Maro' were cheaper than others charging 4d instead of 6d we were not allowed to go to them for fear of bringing home 'visitors'. Fleas and bed bugs were rife.

My musical education had been enjoyable so far, but that changed when Hermione Rowe entered my life.

Chapter 21
Ask Not for Whom the Bell Tolls

Seán's seventh birthday fell on 12th May 1949. His heart's desire had been to get a wind up racing car. As soon as he was dressed he was up at the breakfast table to open his cards and presents, and sure enough there was the blue and yellow racing car. Getting him off to school without the car was a struggle but Granda reasoned with him and eventually persuaded him that Sr. Rita would have better things to do than to admire his car. Gran might as well not have provided a birthday tea since he gobbled everything that was put in front of him, anxious to be out playing and showing off his car. Granda suggested that he should put the key on a piece of string around his neck, but before the Gran had time to open her 'bits of string' tin, he was out the door and off down to the Square. A short time later he was in again bawling his head off complaining that he had lost the key. He was inconsolable.

Granda put on his hat picked up the car and went out. A short time later he was back with the car now modified to be wound up with an old clock winder. Seán was delighted. Gran was pleased 'What made you think of that' she asked. 'There's always more ways than one to skin a cat, he responded smugly. The following morning she was affronted to be told by Irene Fitz that she had seen Granda coming out of 'Uncle's', a source, no doubt, of the clock winder, clocks being a popular item to pawn. However, she never had the opportunity to ask him because he had answered the bell for the ten o'clock Mass, and by mid morning she had other things on her mind. It was Seán who reminded me of this story, telling me he had treasured the car for years.

Friday 13th May was a fine sunny day so Sr.Francis had pulled in the bottom panes of the windows on three sides of the class room with the hooked pole provided. These three enormous windows acted like a glass house in the summer and frosted over with condensation in winter. The sadistic Victorian architect had placed them so that they were too high to look out of, even for an adult. With them open we heard the ambulance bell loud and insistent in the road outside. Sr. Francis went to the windows looking out on St. Agatha's neo roman renaissance style Church, All we could see from our second floor classroom were three statues with clear blue sky behind them balancing on plinths at the top of the front three doored portico. Standing on the hot water pipe that went around the circumference of the room about a foot from the ground, she told us
'Some poor soul has collapsed coming out of the ten o'clock Mass' 'Let's say a prayer for whoever it is' she said as we blessed ourselves to recite the Confiteor.

At the end of the school day Seán was waiting for me at the Boys Entrance. 'That's Granda's hat' he said pointing to a brown fedora hat on the Church railings opposite. We went across and I flicked the hat off the railings with a ruler. It looked like Granda's hat. It has the same kind of leather sweat band as Granda's hat. I smelt it. It smelt of Granda. I took the hat and we ran all the way home. Coming up Empress Place to its junction with Upper Buckingham Street I looked across at the Dwelling's and saw all the drawn blinds. 'Granda's dead' I told Seán, ignoring his rush of questions as we crossed the road and went into the Buildings. Our first floor landing was full of people coming and going and all four flat doors were open and neighbours had brought chairs out into the hall. This communal space was used on such occasions to accommodate baptisms, weddings and, on this occasion, a wake. In the flat Gran was sitting in Granda's chair crying. I was so speechless with fright I didn't know what to do or say. Everything felt strange, even the Gran sitting down, because she was always on her feet. She got up and gave us a hug and said 'Go on over to Annie and she'll give you your tea.

Walking into Annie Lawlor's flat you felt you were likely to meet Queen Victoria. Dark green and brown were the predominant colours, with everything protected by antimacassars. A large aspidistra flourished in a jardinière on a pedestal by the window, which was surprising, since it was constantly in the draft of air from the ever open balcony door. Annie, as roly poly as a firkin always dressed in black. Her hair, scraped back in a bun, still had a lot of its original black, and combined with her sallow skin and dark eyes made you wonder if she had Spanish ancestry. She also has a selection of hairy moles on her chin which I use to try not to look at, and smelled of snuff and Parma violets. Bridie was already at the table red eyed from crying. 'Well now' said Annie closing over the door 'Let's get some food inside yiz' she said ladling rice pudding into three bowls. Being children we not only emptied the bowls but came back for more. Annie Lawlor could bake a great rice pudding, enriched with the top of the milk, raisins, and nutmeg it could have graced the table of the gentry.

'Is Granda dead? I asked, hoping I might have been mistaken because nobody has actually *said* he had died.

'Yes, darling' she said 'He died in the ambulance on his way to 'Jervis Street'.

But, sure isn't it grand that he's gone straight to heaven having only just received the Holy Sacrament and the Last Rites'. I don't think 'grand' was the word that was foremost in our minds so this set the three of us crying our eyes out and the poor woman didn't know what to do with us. The rest of the day was a blur of neighbours coming to offer their condolences and as the four flats became one I was amazed how many people knew him.

The Da and Sheila arrived with the news that there would be a post mortem, so his body would be held at the hospital and would not come home to be Waked. Body or not, people were still coming and going when we went to bed, the men sitting out on the landing drinking to his memory. Seán went to sleep clutching his birthday car for comfort.

Bright and early the following morning the Grans other children, Martin and Tess arrived at the North Wall on the boat from Liverpool. Tess had been living with Martin's family, having gone to Salford to work during the war. With them they had brought Stanley, age eight, one of Martin's children. Having visitors was a great diversion and a novel experience. Stanley's Mancunian accent sounded strange, but he was cheerful, and not the least upset by Granda's death so was good company, particularly for Seán.

On the Sunday Uncle Martin gathered up Éamon and Carol, the three of us and Stan, and took us all to the Pantheon in Talbot Street, one of the few places open on a Sunday, for chips and Italian ice cream. He then walked us over to the Liffey to look at Granda's old tug, and around to Forte's Ice Cream Parlour in O'Connell Street for milk shakes and Coca Cola. With this lethal mixture in my stomach we climbed the 164 spiral steps of Nelson Pillar to step out onto a railed platform to get a bird's eye view of Dublin. My head began to spin, and at the age of ten and a half I discovered I had no head for heights. I leant against the railings and watched my projectile vomit land on the flower sellers below. Before they had time to look up Martin yanked me back out of sight. He may have been in Manchester for fifteen years, but he knew that taking on a bunch of irate Dublin dealers was way out of his league. I don't know what he told them, but we got away unscathed; however I remember him imploring us not to mention it to Gran.

Monday evening, with black arm bands sown on we went to Granda's Vigil in Lourdes, his parish church, and everybody from the Dwellings were there. It was the same for the funeral Mass the following morning. The burial procession then set out for Glasnevin while Bridie, Seán and I made our way to school, yes, school. As far as Gran was concerned we did not need to go to the burial so we should be at school. Our black mourning bands made us the centre of attention, and the recipients of little offerings from sympathetic classmates, so perhaps Gran was right, talking about it among our friends made it feel real. Granda was dead, and he wasn't coming back.

According to his death certificate Granda's post mortem showed he died from myocardial degeneration, what would now be called coronary heart disease. Like a lot of his contemporaries he worked until well into his sixties so enjoyed little or no retirement. To take on the rearing of three young children with seventy-one years behind him and two to go, just when life became a little easier was no mean feat but he accepted it, and us, with good grace. It was many years later that I learned that he and Gran had not raised, Mary Ellen's child Annie. Her childhood and life are shrouded in mystery and there is nobody left to ask.

Granda had been a quiet dignified man, but still well muscled from his time on the tugs. He held his own counsel, but if pushed, the pusher often got more than they expected in debate. He was an articulate self educated man, a Larkinite with a great interest in the International working class movement. He was an unforgiving political opponent hoping that William Martin Murphy was roasting in hell and believed that the participants in the Easter rising in 1916 had scuppered the Home Rule movement led by his namesake. The factional savagery of the Civil War cured him of political involvement and left him with a burning hatred of Dev and Fianna Fáil though a choice of Costello and Fine Gael was equally onerous. The rise of Fascism in the thirties resurrected his Socialist views but by then he was old enough and wise enough to keep them within his own four walls though his heart would have been with the Fifth Brigade. I have no idea what his religious beliefs were apart from observing the Ten Commandments and attending Mass.

Following ten o'clock Mass on weekdays, he kept fit with his daily constitutional along the quays, or down by the canal to sit under the poplars to watch the barges bringing turf in from the bogs. He would stop off for a 'half' at one of his favourite watering holes before going in to Charleville Mall Carnegie Library to read what papers and periodicals were available, or doze by the radiator. I would often pick up Seán at the Bhuachaille school entrance and cross the road to the Library to find Granda so that we could all walk back home together. All three of us children had joined the Library as soon as we could read, and I inherited my love of books from him. Inheriting his Library tickets is another story. He seldom went out in the evening, preferring to stay at home listening to the radio or his gramophone records. He used to joke that he was counting the days before we departed for our summer holidays to Galway. 'Jools' he would say, 'Eight weeks of peace and quiet coming up' 'Sure we won't know ourselves' Gran would say.
'We'll be free as birds from morning till night' he would gloat,
'Well not before….. And the list of jobs she wanted him to do would emerge, and he would sigh and mutter that 'a man's feckin life wasn't his own'. The previous year he had put wall papering

the bedroom 'on the long finger', and now he would never do it. In fact nobody ever changed the fading rambling rose pattern during my childhood. When we went to bed we would drift off to sleep looking at the roses glowing red from the little red lamp under the picture of the Sacred Heart and listening to the murmur of his and Grans voices talking about the events of the day and the 'twish- twish' sounds of shoe cleaning brushes as he polished and buffed all our shoes, a ritual he performed every night. Throughout his marriage Granda had passed his pay packet over to Gran, to be handed back his pocket money while she managed the budget. He never called her to account nor complained about the amount of 'awful' she dished up. His death left a huge hole in our lives. God rest his soul and I hope that wherever he is he is as free as a bird.

Chapter 22
Dya want yer aul lobby washed down?

Annie Lawlor, whose name was always said as if it was one word, was the Gran's neighbour and friend for many years. A widow, in her late sixties her husband Jim had died in 1946 before my siblings and I moved in to the Dwellings. I used to spend weekends with my Grandparents before that so I remember Jim's wake and Annie's ire when he used to chop wood on the landing. Annie was a great character and was fanatical about keeping the landing clean so God forbid that Nick Colgan, the Caretaker, who lived on the ground floor, should dare to check it. Not only did she take her own turn but took on the neighbours rota as well. We had the cleanest landing in the Buildings.

Granda use to say 'tha wan must have feckin shares in Jeyes Fluid' and to this day the smell of Jeyes Fluid conjures up a picture of Annie kneeling on her little rag mat, her buttocks wobbling from side to side, an old flour sack around her waist, scrubbing and humming away. Woe betide any of us children who tried to walk across it before it was dry, and Heaven help the coalman or chisler delivering turf if they left a trail of slack or turf dust behind them.

To the best of my recollection Jim worked as a carter's assistant for Gibney's the Wine Merchants. He loaded casks of Madeira from the docks to be taken by horse and cart to their store house. I think one of the perks was taking home damaged kegs, or perhaps he just liberated them, hence the wood chopping. I remember on one occasion Annie locking him out. The landing door was bolted every night at about 10 o'clock so anybody coming home after that time would expect somebody to stay up and let them in. It became obvious that he had done something to annoy Annie because the whole block was listening to his pleas from the pavement which was falling on deaf ears. He eventually tried to climb in through the half moon space over the landing door and got stuck. By this time we were all up and out on the landing watching the proceedings with a mortified but unmollified Annie shushing him. It ended up in a tug of war with Granda trying to pull him out the way he had climbed in, and Annie pulling him forward. Annie won and he tumbled down on top of her. We were all hysterical with laughter, particularly at Jim trying to plamas Annie. He obviously succeeded because she was cooking him a fry up before we got back to sleep.

Annie, like my Gran had been a seamstress. She was a skilled 'tatter' and made lace collars and antimacassars for a bit of extra money until her eye sight began to fail. In hindsight I'd say she developed cataracts. When my Gran became a widow in '49 she and Annie became very close and we often came home from school to find her sitting by the range. Her door was always open to my brother, sister and me. Whenever I needed peace and quiet to do my homework, or to read, I'd go across the landing to Annie, well wrapped up and with mittens on of course. I often wondered if her obsession with fresh air was TB related, it being part of the cure regime at the time.

She was one of a little band of elderly women in the Buildings who went on wearing the black shawl instead of a coat long after clothing coupons ceased. However she always looked faintly comical because she wore a hat with it that the Granda used to describe as 'like a pillbox on an elephants head'.

In the early sixties I took Gran to see the film of Mary Poppins, and as Mary descended from the heavens the people around us were treated to her amused response. As Mary had hove into view the Gran had exclaimed 'Holy Mother a God, yer wan is wearing

Annie Lawlor's hat'. Annie's sight was then too bad for her to enjoy 'going to the pictures'. Her pleasures were easily satisfied with a twist of 'British Empire' mixture snuff and a tin of Parma Violets. Annie was a good neighbour and a great wit. Throughout my teenage years she remained part of my life and I remember her with great affection.

I always took note of her sagacious reminder to me to carry 'mad' money.

'Don't be dependent on any louser seeing you home; always stick your fare home in your bra if you're going on a date'.

Advice that stood me in good stead on a couple of occasions!

Chapter 23
Nymphs and Shepherds

Following Granda's death, Tess, then aged twenty four, moved in with us. She got a job in Armstrong's print works in Amien Street giving up her job in an electrical engineering factory in Salford. She had worked there throughout the war fitting asbestos linings to ceramic relay equipment, a factor implicated in her death in 1985. Apart from that life continued as before. We visited Granda's grave frequently. He was buried in the same grave as my mother so we split the flowers between them and prayed for both of them.

1951 and having spent the autumn term in Claregalway School improving my Irish for the Scholarship Viva I returned to North William Street in the New Year to find that civil war had broken out. During the Christmas Masses Sr. Kevin had been very terse with us so I tried to find out what was going on. We're not sure' Mary Bennett and Bernie Moran told me in whispered conclave in the corner of the school yard, 'but there's Holy War going on between her and Miss Rowe. Miss Hermione Rowe taught the parallel class to Sr. Francis, so between them they taught about seventy children.

When Tess heard that Miss Rowe was still teaching at the school she couldn't believe it. 'She must be eighty if she's a day' she said in amazement 'I had her twelve years ago, and she was in her dotage then', she said. Miss Rowe had an interest in singing, and after four years with her class she had a nice tidy little choir. However there was a big Ard Ceoil coming up and she wanted to enter a *school* choir for it. Even a twelve year old could see that this would have Sr. Kevin and her reefing each other's hair out, if

Sr. Kevin had had any hair to reef out (Nuns been shorn in case you didn't know).

Miss Rowe's argument was that Sr. Kevin didn't even *teach* in the girl's school and already had the church choir to keep her busy. Sr. Kevin's argument was that the girls in her church choir all attended the school and had been trained by her, therefore if North William Street was entering a choir it should be hers. Sr. Monica, sensible woman that she was, sent it to Mother Provincial for adjudication. Miss Rowe won, and that should have been the end of it, but she cherry picked those of us she wanted from the church choir. Sr. Kevin retaliated by holding her rehearsals at the same time. This resulted in about a dozen of us having to take sides, so we stayed with Sr. Kevin. Eventually sanity reigned and we were free to attend Miss Rowe's rehearsals but she had marked our cards. We didn't give a shoite because we were never going to have her as a teacher.
Oh, my God how wrong we were!

Fair play to her she was a good singing teacher and her class could harmonise better than we, in the church choir, could. The two songs chosen for the Feis were 'Nymphs and Shepherds' for diction and harmony, and 'Oro se do Bheatha aBhaile' to show that Dev's compulsory Irish was having some effect. I had known the latter song for years having sung it often to shorten the journey down the long bog road during the summer holidays. The problem was I had learned it in 'quick march time' so was always at least two syllables ahead of everyone else. My other problem was being put next to anybody who was singing a different part of the harmony because I couldn't concentrate on my part without putting my fingers in my ears, an idiosyncrasy Miss Rowe quickly cured with a rap on the head with her baton.

The competition was somewhere huge, probably Ballsbridge.

A coach was hired for first thing one Saturday morning, and sick with excitement we set off accompanied by Miss Rowe, Sr. Francis, Sr. Monica, and Sr. Kevin who had made peace with her arch rival. None of us having a decent school uniform we were told to ask our mammies to make sure our frocks were blue. Woolworths must have run out of blue dye that week with mothers dunking multicoloured frocks in vats of dye. Between Sr. Monica not specifying what colour blue she was expecting, and the underlying colour of the garment influencing the result, we were a motley crew who set off. My dyed aquamarine taffeta Confirmation dress developed a life of its own as it shimmered and flickered in its new electric blue tinge. We'd have been much better off wearing our Sunday best. When we got to the venue we were struck dumb by the size of it and the number of children there. We were also green with envy when we saw the posh uniforms of some of the other choirs. We seemed so out of place and some of them actually laughed at us.

Sr. Monica gathered us round her and jerked her head at a group looking down their noses at us.

'That lot are from the Loreto College in Foxrock' she said 'And you're as good as any of them.'

While she nodded coolly to the Loreto Sister in charge of them, we fell about the place laughing at the mere idea, but when they got up on the podium to sing we looked at each other with satisfaction and knew we could wipe the floor with them. We were eliminated after singing in three rounds and reaching the top ten. We came nowhere near the prizes but it was reward enough to know we had beaten Foxrock.

Chapter 24
The Mot

1951 had been an eventful year. We had been living happily with the Gran for nearly five years and spending summers with the Ma's family in Galway. I was in my thirteenth year and thought I knew everything, Bridie was eleven, amenable and quiet, and asking for bullying, while Seán at nine was everyone's little darling. Little did the Gran know that he was quite the little grifter. Gran never went into our cardboard boxes under the bed which held what few treasures we had, but one day I was looking for something and not finding it looked first in Bridie's box where I found several hair slides belonging to me, and then in Seán's.

Seán's box bore dire warnings on the top, bottom and all four sides, 'Keep out,' 'Private',' Enter and die', 'Danger, you've been warned' 'Trespassers beware' and a skull and crossbones for good measure. 'Well, I thought, the little git's spelling can't be faulted' but what the hell is in here? It seemed to be just full of his Eagle and Rover comics, conkers, marbles and other little boy treasures, when down at the bottom inside a sock (that the Gran had gone hairless trying to match up) I found a packet of Woodbines, matches and a bag of three penny pieces. What in the name of God was he up to? It would break Gran's heart if she found out he was smoking or stealing. We had just celebrated the New Year and were still off school so I went out looking for him.

There was neither hide nor hair of him to be found, all his friends responding with shuffling guilt. It was one of Bridie's clique who told me 'He's up at the Turf Depot', so over I went to the 27 Steps, and there was your man standing beside our old pram while little Eric Breslin, his freckles standing out like measles on his white skin, loaded it with a second bag of turf. The Breslin kids, like us, had very fair skin. You could always recognise them because they were as speckled as starlings. My little goody two shoes brother tried to bluff it out saying they were only helping out poor aul widows who had nobody to bring home their turf.

When I told him I had found his stash he was full of righteous indignation about the invasion of his privacy, but when I threatened to box his ears if he didn't shut up and tell me what was going on, I got the story.

He had being going up to the Da's and getting the pram out of the shed, hiring it out to other kids who used it to deliver turf. He was taking a percentage of their earnings and with this money he had been buying packets of Woodbines and boxes of matches. He was then selling the fags individually with a free match thrown in, and undercutting local tobacconists. I couldn't believe the ingenuity of the conniving little brat and could have kicked myself for not thinking of it, at least the pram deal.

Grans birthday was on the twenty seventh of January. I made him spend his ill gotten gains on a brooch from all three of us. Gran was very touched believing we had been saving up our pocket money. We never disillusioned her.

The events of a few months later soon banished my brother's entrepreneurial scams from my mind.

I had been aware that there was a lot of low toned conversations between Gran, Sheila and Tess that ended abruptly when I came into earshot, and assumed it was about 'women things' and had something to do with the mysterious death of one of the Breslin girls. But the Dwellings looked after its own, and while there might have been plenty of speculation behind closed doors about Bridget's death none of us children got to know the details for several years when the trial of Mamie Cadden came before the Courts.

I was therefore amazed when out playing 'two balls' with Bridie Fitz to have her ask me 'What do you think of your Da's mot'? D'ya think you'll get a new Mammy'?

Picking my jaw up off the ground I asked her what the hell she was talking about. She told me she has overheard her Ma and May Grant gossiping. Apparently my Da was going out with a 'young wan' who worked in Dooley's shop on the corner of Summerhill Place. I was agog with curiosity and indignation, and set out to find out what was going on. Apparently it was true. He was 'walking out' with a twenty year old country girl, and was the talk of the Buildings. Although the shop was within spitting distance Gran never darkened its doorstep because it was owned by hard headed culchies, and run by a manager who wasn't free to negotiate prices, so we had no excuse to go in and look at 'yer wan'.

I gave him the third degree when he came to tea on the Saturday and he tried to weasel out of it saying it was early days. I don't know what his mother and sisters said to him but vibes said they thought he was making an eejit of himself. Sheila was beside herself with scorn 'When I think that yer man had the cheek to call Christy a cradle snatcher because he was twelve years older than me, and now *he's* carrying on with a *culchie* young enough to be his daughter'. 'He's making a Holy Show of himself and the family'. The latter was a cardinal sin in a respectable family. With the National Primary Exam coming up in May I gave his 'walking out' little thought, and was relieved when the results came out in June to find that I'd passed. Although the school leaving age was fourteen years, employers would employ you if you had good

Primary Examination results, so some girls knew they would be in the workplace before the summer holidays were over.

Chapter 25

The Ciotóg

We went off to Galway for the summer and came home to be told that the Da had got married. All we were concerned about was how it was going to affect us. 'You'll stay here' Gran said 'Sure yer wan couldn't be left in charge of an ice cream cornet'. The Da had done it again. This time he had married '*yer wan,*' the first time it had been '*that woman.* However this was mild in comparison to Martin's wife Lucy who was known as 'the Proxy Doxie'. I learned a long time later that Betty had married the Da over her mother Annie's 'dead body' and that they didn't speak for years. By waiting for her twenty first birthday she was able to marry without parental consent.

Even with the scholarship exam looming, I was counting the days waiting for the holidays to end to return to school for my final year.

We formed our line in the school yard and filed up the stairs behind Sr. Francis. No talking was allowed on the stairs so we waited until the classroom door was closed before erupting and disgorging our pent up holiday news to each other, and to Sr. Francis. She let us continue until an uneasy silence was reached because usually, by then, she would have called for quiet. We looked at her and knew that bad news was coming. She didn't have to ask for our attention, every eye was fixed on her.

'Sr. Monica has asked me to tell you that I won't be teaching you this year'

There was stunned silence. Then pandemonium before she could say more. Eventually we learned that there were not enough girls to warrant two leaving classes, so we were being amalgamated with Miss Rowe's class, and Miss Rowe would be our teacher. Holy Mother of Christ, *was she serious?*

Those of us in the choir looked at each other in horror. Sr. Francis chose to ignore the audible blasphemy that was coming from every corner. Those who weren't blaspheming were already crying and I soon joined them. We could see that Sr. Francis was upset too, and when she told us she had to go and take over her new class we felt totally abandoned. She asked us to be good until Sr. Monica collected us, and to do our best in Miss Rowe's class.
Poor Sr. Monica took the brunt of our outrage when she came through the door. She could cane the whole lot of us as far as we were concerned. We'd never actually seen her cane but had it on good authority that she had one in her office. Muffing her hands in her long wide sleeves she reiterated what Sr. Francis had told us, and also explained that the reason Miss Rowe was chosen for the amalgamated class was because Sr. Francis had started on another five year stint with one of the current First Communion classes, and Miss Rowe wouldn't be around to do that again. Feck the Communion Class, feck Miss Rowe, and why the feck hadn't she retired already? Of course we didn't actually *say* any of this as we formed a surly line to be taken over to Miss Rowe's class at the back of the school. Hermione Rowe was ready for us.

A well preserved spinster of uncertain age, with a devotion to the Irish Girl Guides and the remote Fr Newth, she stood there in her sturdy shoes, tweed shirt, twinset and pearls.
'You will find your name on an allocated desk' she said 'please take your seats quietly' she ordered, looking over her glasses at us. The devil incarnate had pre selected our seats, interspersing us between 'her girls' so that none of us sat next to each other. Sr. Monica left us to our fate.   I was to share a desk with Mary Bennett. I was now in the second desk, row two, to the left of

Hermione's desk. Behind me Bernie Moran whispered despairingly into the upturned top of her desk.

'Holy Mother of God we're doomed'.

She got no further as the hawk like head of our nemesis raked the room with its 360 degree swivel.

'Get your books out for Dictation' she said.

Pacing up and down she dictated several sentences before stopping at my desk. I thought she was going to praise my neat perfectly formed hand writing when she said

'There are no 'ciotgachs' in my class, put the pen in your right hand'.

I pointed out to her that I had always been allowed to write with my left hand and couldn't now unlearn it.

'Oh, you will' she said grimly, 'you will'. 'I won't correct anything you write with your left hand' she said as her stony grey eyes tried to rivet me to the spot.

A rage rose inside me and memories of a bullying priest in Claregalway who had tried to coerce me into chasing golf balls down a field to facilitate his putting practice (another story, another Memoir) came rushing back, and I knew within myself, that even if this woman cut of my left hand she'd never make me write with the other. I was determined to stand my ground. Gran use to say of me 'Youze could hang draw and quarter that wan, grind her into mince and she'd still be spittin back at youze from the frying pan'. The standoff went on for days until I told Tess, who had been one of 'Miss Rowe's girls'. Initially she didn't believe me but I showed her the uncorrected work. However even she hadn't got the gumption to go up and confront her, so resurrecting Granda's maxim that 'there's more than one way to skin a cat' took the problem to Sr. Monica. Sr. Monica came up to the classroom the following morning and told me quietly to bring my books to an empty desk at the back then sat down beside me and went through them. I didn't dare look at Miss Rowe but I could feel her eyes boring holes in me, and I wondered why I wasn't dropping dead on the spot.

'Go back to your desk Bernadette' Sr. Monica told me.

No *Bernadette Mary* so I wasn't in trouble.

She and Miss Rowe left the room, the latter returning with a neck like a turkey cock.

'Pick up your pen and get on with your work' she told me.

'With my left hand or my right hand' I asked?

For one minute I thought she was going to hit me, but she didn't, and to give her due I never saw her slap anybody.

    She was a competent teacher, and 'her girls' had never known anything different, but Sr. Francis girls knew what it was like to have had a great teacher. However there is no denying Hermione excelled in intimidation, a type of bullying that would have crushed a less resilient child. She could sniff out fear like a bloodhound. I worked consciously in her class, primarily because I wanted to be one step ahead of her if she ever threw a question my way; she never did, nor did I ever speak to her unless she spoke to me first. It was a game of 'one-upmanship' and I learned to be a worthy antagonist. Like the late Canon Moran her vindictiveness gave me a good grounding in dealing with bullies.

I learned that while I might have been prepared to die bullies couldn't kill me and God did not strike you dead if you stood up to them. Anything else was a bonus and I knew that showing a bit of gumption was half the battle. Granda's maxim was that gumption was not something you licked it off the stones!

My unflinching pigheadedness is in the Redmond Norman warrior genes though you'd never think it from the family motto which is a wishy-washy; 'Live piously and love God and country'!

Chapter 26

Exodus

The new Mammy, ten years older than me, set about making a home in Upper Rutland Street. The Da made the mistake of saying to me 'Now that you have a new Mammy how do you feel about coming home'?

I pointed out that while he might have a new *wife*, I most certainly did not have a new *Mammy*, and my home was in the Buildings. Bridie and Seán were easier fodder and while they never called Betty anything but Betty they moved back leaving me with Gran 'until I had come to my senses'. Hell would freeze over first. As I'm writing this the Da would be a hundred years old today. We never had an easy relationship so whenever I came home from London I would go to see him, promising myself that I would not argue with him, but five minutes in his company I would find myself taking a stance on anything, whether it was contrary to my beliefs, historical accuracy or common sense, just for the gratification of disagreeing with him. With the family decanted to a newly built suburb of Kilmore in Coolock I'd look up at the heavens and see the Aer Lingus Viscounts' flying out of Collinstown, and feel for my return ticket in my pocket, and think 'one hour away is sanity'.

Having been a reluctant father during our childhood he and Betty adopted four great kids, and although he still kept up some Union activities he was home by his own fireside most evenings. He had a massive heart attack when he was about sixty five and I was just about to book a flight home from London when Betty phoned to tell me he had walked out of the Coronary Care Unit and was at home. He was told to pack in the cigarettes, give up the booze, and retire. To prove the medical profession wrong he did none of these things and went on to live another ten years to spite them. I last saw him on his seventy third birthday. I was going to work in the Philippines for two years so came over especially to see him and make my peace with him. While we had the opportunity to talk we kept our reminiscing to safe subjects, resolving nothing, but leaving me with a less judgmental view of him. His humorous parting remark, accompanied by a brief hug, was 'Well, I suppose I'll be dead by the time you come again'. *My* retort was 'Well I'm certainly not laying out the fare to come back from the Philippines for your funeral, so you'd better hang on'. But like Granda when his time came eleven months later, he just keeled over and died, in the North Side Shopping Centre. My first reaction was 'Why the hell hadn't he gone on living to spite *me,* it had worked with the doctors'? He was days buried before I heard the news. He had never been the best father in the world but I suppose he had done his best, and that is all we should ask of our parents.

The Gran went on living in the Dwellings until the early seventies. One of her idiosyncrasies was her attitude to the television, in particular Charles Michel reading the news. She behaved as if he was only talking to her. She would prepare for his presence by taking off her pinny and tidying her hair. The table would be cleared and her chair plonked in front of the tele as if she was in the front row stalls. She would keep up a running commentary in response to his items of news;
'Is that so?'
'Well would you believe it?'
'Isn't it well for her'!
'Mudder a God'!
'The Lord between us and all harm'!
'The poor unfortunate'!

'The Lord preserve us'!

I remember on one occasion unfolding the clothes horse in front of the fire and hanging some underwear on it to air. It was in full view of Charles so her castigation was prolonged and her mortification unappeased.

It brought to mind the Radio Eireann call signal of old. Whenever there was an interval between programmes that needed to be filled, instead of playing music as is common today, on many occasions the Station would simply play the Identification Signal 'O'Donnell Abu' until it was time to introduce the next programme. This evocative two minute call sign was like a time clock in our childhood and was as familiar as 'The Angelus'.

According to RTE Archives the electro-mechanical cylinder, which sounded like a nineteenth century music box or an early 1920s pianola, consisted of a revolving brass cylinder about 5 inches in diameter with a series of short thin steel pegs inserted at timed intervals around its circumference. When set in motion electrically the device caused the pegs to strike or pluck flexible steel strips which were cut to exact musically resonant lengths. The vibrations of each strip produced the notes of the tune. However the Gran was totally convinced that some lonely little man sat in a room on the third floor of the GPO in Henry Street, home of Radio Éireann, playing it over and over on a glockenspiel. 'God love him, he never gets a note wrong' she would say in appreciation.

Most of the old neighbours, relics of aul decency, including Annie Lawlor were dead, and a lot of their children had moved away but 'Mrs. Redmond' at No.31 was well known to those who remained. In her early nineties it was still impossible to get her to take the weight of her feet and she would scuttle about doing her shopping, but now only venturing up to Summerhill.

As well as the television she had always been eccentric about the use of electricity, believing that empty light sockets leaked electricity, and she wouldn't use an electric iron in case she got a shock ironing damp clothes. At a time when wall mounted sockets were a thing of the future in the Dwellings, irons were plugged into the overhead light socket with the aid of an adapter, so she was quite right to be cautious because the socket had no earth. Radios and televisions had to be plugged in in the same fashion, but had built in aerials which could be attached to an earth hanging out the window and clipped to a metal pin. At some point the Dwellings were rewired and the ranges taken out but Gran went on using her old cast iron irons, spitting on the base to gauge how hot it was. The family began to notice how forgetful she was becoming, but it was her neighbours who alerted them to the fact that she was going out at night thinking she was going to her ten o'clock mass. However it was the ironing that gave her away. With her range gone she heated the irons on the Mersey gas stove and kept forgetting about them, or else forgot to check the heat so that the amount of scorched clothes grew. She eventually became too confused to live alone so moved out to the Tonlegee Road to shared care at the homes of Sheila and Tess. Eventually she needed nursing care and settled in to Sr. Claire's where she died age 93y in 1975. When the family cleared the flat we found she had paid for all our funerals on her penny policies. I had a letter from the Prudential on my sixtieth birthday informing me that my policy had reached maturity in the princely sum of £81. 91. When she took it out in 1938 the average cost of a funeral was £30. She was a great woman, or as her neighbours described her, 'a dacent little body'. We owe her a great debt of gratitude. Her legacy to us was her ten commandments.

Always wear clean underwear

Always carry a safety pin
Never stare at people – it's rude
Never eat in the street
Never swim on a full stomach
Never leave the house with wet hair
Never spend money you don't have
Never take rubies from swine
Civility costs nothing
Whatever else you lose keep your dignity.

I was going to say 'God give her peace' but knowing her propensity for striking bargains perhaps it's God who needs the peace!

The slum clearances of the fifties moved the old Gardiner Estate neighbourhoods to far flung corners of a greener Dublin in Ballymun, and Ballyfermot leaving the Artisans' Dwellings behind. The 'Hoors' in City hall tore down rows of seedy Georgian and Regency Terraces, and Squares, until protests were raised in the sixties, by which time it was far too late. The Corporation then knocked the guts out of the Summerhill putting up the ticky tacky gerry built, ironically named, Mountain View flats. By the '80's the area was notorious for cheap heroin, drug pushers and gangsters and the flats had reverted to slums. The Dwellings were taken over by a private landlord and renovated to within an inch of their life. Security doors were installed, the Blocks were surrounded by six foot railings and the façade plastered with lilac Santex ten times worse than the scutter yellow landing walls ever were! The Square and the Terrace turned in to a gated area. I was going to say 'community' but that was the one thing it ceased to be.

While the new suburbs gave people better housing they were little more than concrete jungles with no schools, churches or pubs, little or no public transport and imprisoned women in their new four bedroom homes behind their own front doors and letterboxes. The camaraderie, the support of neighbours and doorstep gossip was gone, to be replaced with bathrooms, gardens, open spaces and uprooted unhappy children wanting their old gangs and muckers. Eventually, like the earlier development of Drumcondra, Cabra and Crumlin trees grew, the infrastructure improved, children found new ways of getting into trouble and developed new loyalties. But for those of us reared in Dublin 1 our nostalgia for the old way of life remained and is best summed up by Paul St. John's 'Rare Auld times' ;

'Raised on songs and stories

Heroes of renown

The passing tales of glory

That once was Dublin Town

The hallowed halls and houses

The haunting children's rhymes

That once was Dublin City in the rare auld times.

~ ~ ~ ~

OTHER MEMOIRS by the same Author;

The Summer Children

Thrown on Life's Surge

Pea Soup and Jellied Eels

A Promise of Tomorrows

THE SUMMER CHILDREN

Chapter 1

The Road from Dublin

The long car journey was nearly over. Our driver, Christy Clinton, who bore a passing resemblance to Humphrey Bogart, was as unperturbed and cheerful as when we had left Dublin seven hours earlier. The 126 Irish miles to Co. Galway, with stops to enable my father to indulge in liquid refreshment, and us children to explore the revolting 'toilet' facilities in bona fide hostelries, would not have taken the average car driver seven hours in 1944, but Uncle Christy, a year married to the Da's sister, Sheila, was no ordinary driver. He considered himself a good driver, a careful driver, a courteous driver, but to every other driver on the road he was a menace, implanting murderous impulses in their hearts and creating red mists of rage to cloud their powers of rational thought.

Uncle Christy was probably the originator of road rage. When he drove, he took up pole position in the middle of the road, progressing at a stately twenty five miles an hour in his shiny black 1938 Ford Fordor car , never overtaking or pulling over, ever mindful of wandering sheep and cattle, suicidal dogs, horse and carts, hay laden tractors, the lame and the halt, the mad, the bad and the sad and sundry other hazards that might require an emergency stop. Not that he ever had to make a emergency stop, due to his hyper vigilance we always has plenty of time to come to a rolling halt. In concentrating on driving with due care and attention he happily ignored the orchestra of honking horns and the curses of fellow road users who cut in, or overtook him, and he seemed oblivious to the sins of blasphemy he was responsible for, from normally reasonable and easy going Irish drivers. What any of us were doing driving across Éire, as it was then called, where strict rationing was in force, was not a question that interested a young child.

As the grandeur of the Claregalway Friary ruins came into view my heart began to race, and my stomach tie itself in knots of anticipation. We came up to the turn for Cloonbiggen and the sight of the De Burgo keep on the far shore of the River Clare revealed itself. The sun broke forth after a passing shower it throwing out the colours of golden lichen clothing its grey time-beaten stones, contrasting with the dark green of the ivy that wandered up its walls and around its windows and corbelled parapet and the brilliant green of the umbelliferous plants that clustered around its feet. It vied in its feudal beauty in harmony of colour and form with the ecclesiastical ruins facing it.

The car turned right onto the bog road putting the Friary on our left and as it rocked and jolted along this rutted sun dried boreen, my eyes were on the flat horizon ahead, and the enormous blue sky with its occasional thin wispy cirrus cloud. We passed the Connell's farmhouse on the right and saw Maggie in the yard turning to look at the unusual sight of a car down in Cloonbiggen. Doctor, Priest, soldier, the select groups allowed a petrol ration, the query was in her stance as she put up her hand to shade her eyes, but the grapevine had been busy, and as she recognized us, she waved.

At the fork in road we passed the Holland's, turned right and were then hemmed in by the fuchsia bushes and uncut hawthorns, blackthorns and brambles that hid my grandmothers small thatched cottage from view until we pulled up outside. But I had smelt it before I caught a glimpse of the house, the turf fire.

When I would return to Dublin in eight weeks time my clothes and belongings would be impregnated with that musty earthy smell, and despite my mother's attempts to eradicate it with lavender bags, and eucalyptus leaves from the Botanical Gardens it would cling on in my Sunday best woolen coat well up to Christmas Mass.

As we slowed down, a black and white collie came from nowhere and tried to bite lumps out of Christy's tires. For a man who had calmly and serenely, driven across Éire, no culchie cur was going to destroy *his* tyres, so he leapt out of the car like a man possessed, forgetting as he did so to engage the handbrake.

Luckily our screams woke my befuddled father who managed to halt the car inches from a three foot ditch draining the meadow opposite the house. The dog vanished.

THROWN ON LIFE'S SURGE

Chapter 1

With the chimes of the New Year of 1956 a little more than nine hours old Christy Clinton drove at a stately pace across the City on New Year's morning to the leafy south Dublin suburb of Ranlagh with its tree lined streets and grand Victorian mansions and lesser statused Edwardian villas. Turning down Northbrook Road on that bleak January morning I pointed out to him the Hospital on one side of the road with the Nurses Home opposite. His wife, my Aunt Sheila had come along out of a burning curiosity to have a look around. This was well cloaked as concern for my welfare on leaving home for the first time. While he grappled with my suitcase, Sheila, dressed to the nines, sailed up the front steps of a big semi-detached Victorian residence with me at her heels. The door bell was answered by a young girl in a blue serge dress who bobbed at Sheila and bypassing the front room to the right, showed us into a parlour overlooking a substantial lawned garden. A small consumptive looking elderly nun entered before we even had time to sit down. She looked overwhelmed by the Daughter of Charity of St. Vincent de Paul long blue wide sleeved habit, and its soaring seagull type head dress. However, frail as she looked she had Christy and Sheila on their way home within five minutes just giving Christy enough time to transfer two folded pound notes into my hand as he winked goodbye.

Such was my meeting with Sr. Agnes who was in charge of housekeeping as well as the hospital sewing room and laundry. The latter task was not as burdensome as it might seem since the bulk of the washing and ironing was farmed out to the penitents at the nearest Magdalene Laundry.

'I have arranged for Nurse Donovan to be your guide for the next few days'. 'She will be here soon' she said gesturing for me to follow her up the grand staircase to a first floor bedroom overlooking the tree lined road.

I lugged my suitcase up the stairs bumping it several times which elicited a couple of winces from Sr. Agnes but no reprimand. The room looked like a small ward with a bed in each corner. It smelt of sweaty shoes. A Holy picture graced each wall as well as a notice which read. 'It is forbidden to eat or store food in bedrooms. It attracts vermin'. There were curtains on a track that completely surrounded each bed. 'For modesty' explained Sr. Agnes. I was thinking more of privacy myself. All the curtains were neatly pulled back 'And are only to be pulled if you are undressing or going to bed' she said. Besides a bed each of the four occupants has a chest of drawers, a chair, small wardrobe and attached to the wall a wooden rack with five pegs. From three of the sets of pegs a variety objects hung but before I could scrutinise them Sr. Agnes explained 'They are for your towel, sponge bag, shoe cleaning kit, dressing gown and personal laundry bag'. 'They are most certainly *not* for drying your stockings' she said emphatically, glancing at the rack behind me on which hung four long black offenders 'You will find a small drying room in the basement and a Dutch airer in the bathroom she went on 'And there are sufficient hangers in your wardrobe and space in your drawers for all your possessions so there is no excuse for untidiness.

For several minutes I'd being saying 'Yes, Sister' 'Yes, Sister' like a demented mynah bird. She suddenly stopped talking and looked at me until she had my full attention.

'You've not been away from home before' she half stated, half asked in a kindly tone.

'No, Sister' I responded somewhat puzzled.
'Well Nurse, in time you'll find that while some would say that cleanliness is next to Godliness when you live communally tidiness is equally important. It shows consideration for those who have to clean up after you'.

Most of what she had said I had somehow absorbed, but rational thought has ceased when she called me Nurse. Reality set in. On the foot of the bed in the left hand corner away from the window was a stack of neatly folded uniform and on top was a large folded blue and white striped drawstring bag made from the same material as the dresses, and clearly marked Nurse B M Redmond.

'Let me go through your uniform with you, before I leave you to Nurse Donovan' she said going over to the pile.
She made an inventory checking that everything had been brought across from her domain in the hospital sewing room.

4 dresses
6 starched collars
2 white grosgrain belts
8 starched aprons
2 starched caps
Navy cloak
Small box with studs, safety pins, and hooks and eyes

I had been pre fitted for the uniform at interview so in theory it should fit me. Sr. Agnes left me with instructions to sew name tapes on to all uniform items before sending them to be laundered, and to unpack and bring my case to the basement Trunk Room where it would be locked away. Theresa Donovan later told me caustically 'They don't want you keeping it under the bed in case you do a midnight flit'. I was more charitable and believed it was to make life easier for the cleaner who had to buff our lino covered floors.

PEA SOUP AND JELLIED EELS

Chapter 1
Circling the Drain

Following my journey across the Irish Sea on the B&I Ferry, the Hibernia, and a six hour journey on the Holyhead to Euston Mail Train I sat stupefied with tiredness in the tube longing for a peaceful death. I had been met at the barrier by a dumpy, sullen, monosyllabic student nurse, who had been picked on by an all powerful Home Sister to meet the train and deliver me in one piece to her office. Overawed and apprehensive I followed her meekly down into the bowels of the earth taking a seat beside her on the Circle Line Tube. I expected my first Underground journey to Bromley-by-Bow to be brief and uneventful and estimated that a further 15 minutes travel wouldn't kill me.
'Seven stops to Tower Hill' she volunteered. I nodded, too tired to talk. I fell to reading the strip of advertising panels above the heads of the passengers opposite me. Interspersed by maps of the route and 'No Spitting' signs I learned that;
'Rip Van Winkle fell asleep
It was a longish snooze
His clothes indeed were sadly worn but not his Rebuilt Shoes'.
~

'No home remedy or quack doctor ever cured syphilis or gonorrhoea.
Seek free confidential advice at the Middlesex Clinic'.
~

North, South, East or West, Fry's Cocoa is the best'.
~

'Don't be a Fool do Littlewoods Pools'

Eventually my eyes drifted up to the route map opposite just as we came in to Notting Hill Station.
There was definitely something wrong here.

The Circle line was built to join up the main railway termini and had 27 stations on its circular route and was the favourite line, and home-from-home for twenty hours a day of the homeless and dispossessed. Most of its route, and all of the stations, are shared by either the District, Hammersmith & City and Metropolitan lines so getting off at Tower Hill and hopping on the District Line to take us further East we should by now have been alighting at Bromley-by-Bow.

'We're going the wrong way round' I told my surly companion whose head was buried in a 'Woman's Own' she had found abandoned on an empty seat. If she had said anything besides 'Oh crumbs' I might have considered forgiving her but my prolonged muttered blasphemous response would have had my Guardian Angel shocked to the core and kept a priest busy for a week deciding on a penance. I later learned it was her day off and that she had not been a willing volunteer.

I had chosen to train at St. Andrews Hospital E3 as a result of a recruitment drive by English hospital Matrons who were in Dublin seeking girls willing to train as State Registered Nurses. I knew that if I applied to any Irish Hospital to do my General Training I would have to pay £200 for the privilege. In the United Kingdom I would be trained free *and* get a salary. Coming to the end of a year's pre training course at St. Anne's Skin and Cancer Hospital I was persuaded by a fellow nurse, Rita Carroll to accompany her to various Dublin hotel lounges to let the Matrons give us the once over. Armed with our training

Schedules we presented ourselves for interrogation and scrutiny while consuming the coffee and biscuits provided at each venue. All four Matrons we saw offered us a place 'subject to completion of our course and acceptance by their hospital's Board of Governors', the latter I knew was a mere formality if Matron had given us the nod. It was gratifying and a huge relief to realise our General training was assured. Our futures could be in Birmingham, Liverpool, London or Manchester. Both Rita and I had been very taken by Grace Laing, the Matron from St. Andrew's in London's East End. Sitting with her and three other possible recruits in Wynn's Hotel I felt she was the only one who had shown a genuine interest in our individual backgrounds and reasons for emigrating. It was also reassuring to be told that she had several ex Probationers from St.Anne's in training and that half of her trained staff was Irish, so Carroll and I both registered an interest in joining the 1957 January set.

What we didn't know at the time was that a goodly proportion of the Sisters appointed before her tenure were less than happy with her views on improving the Hospital regime and Nurse Training, and of foraging for potential recruits in Ireland and the Dominions. Nearer home her tendency to choose candidates with character and potential meant giving opportunities to girls who had had to leave school without formal qualifications due to the drudgery of family duties. She had to get the Board of Governors on side to do so but since her choices proved their worth she usually got her way.

What I did know was that I was part of a generation whose future would be on a foreign shore. Ireland, an impoverished country with a dismal economic environment and De Valera's deeply conservative theocratic government would not be able to meet either our aspirations or expectations in the furtherance of a career. Our exodus was rationalized by many families as a temporary expedient until things improved at home but I was realistic enough to know that my exile would be a long one.

When I informed Sister Mary Joseph, Reverent Mother and Matron at St. Anne's, that I had chosen St. Andrews as a training hospital she vented her displeasure in no uncertain terms. She was convinced I would come to a bad end, be 'led astray', might even stop going to Mass or worse still, might marry some heathen in a registry office and be damned for ever; that would be nearly as bad as staying at home and marrying a protestant.

I fulfilled her worst nightmares.

A PROMISE OF TOMORROW

Chapter 1
Wild life in SE 21

Two pair of eyes stared unblinkingly at me seated on one of the back side seats of a battered twelve seater yellow Bedford van. They knelt facing me on the middle seat to scrutinize me in comfort. My month old daughter slept in her bassinette beside me while on the opposite seat a carrycot held an eight month baby, arms above his head and dead to the world apart from the occasional gentle sucking movements he made with his mouth. 'Sit down' the driver said firmly to the kneeling children, who totally ignored her. 'I only brought three of them in case you changed your mind if you met them en masse' she said cheerfully looking back at me through the van mirror.

My new employer, Ann, was a well built, bohemian looking woman, with hair twisted into an untidy bun, a face free of any trace of makeup and full of character rather than beauty. A doctor, with five children under ten, she handled the cumbersome van expertly and without apparent effort on our journey from Harrow-on-the-Hill to West Dulwich.

I had previously been to the Dulwich house to be interviewed so knew what to expect. On that occasion the three older children had been in Sussex with their grandmother and the younger ones sleeping. Shabby and untidy the house had seemed quiet and peaceful. My daughter and I would be expected to live en famille with me employed as 'mothers help'. My room on the second floor was spacious and warm and overlooked the road and obliquely, Dulwich College Prep School. I would share this landing with Jane age four and, John, the baby who was currently sleeping in the dressing room adjacent to his parent's bedroom would join us as soon as I had settled in. There was bathroom across the landing, a single bedroom converted into a kitchen and two double bedrooms, one housing Jane. Peter, father of the children, had been inveigled out of his study near the end of the interview to give me the once over. A thin dark haired man in a leg iron, and also a doctor, he scrutinized me as thoroughly as his children were now doing. 'Your application makes you sound as if you can do everything apart from walk on water' he said humorously. 'Well, given time I'll probably master that too' I responded smartly much to his amusement. His easy charm and droll sense of humour immediately put me at ease but disconcerted Ann because he began regaling me with horror stories about previous employees who had fled unable to cope with their children's unruly behaviour, and the lack of routine and consistently in the household.

A small grimy hand held out a match box towards me and said invitingly 'Would you like to see inside?' I saw the glint of devilment in the eyes of the grubby handed blonde eight year old and remembered my Cousin Tommy Duggan's frog collection. 'Ok, let's have a look' I said encouragingly. With his thumb he gently pushed the matchbox open while holding it out in my direction. Much to his disappointment the ensuing screams were not from me but from the four year old Jane who took a flying leap into one of the front passenger seats of the van causing her mother to veer wildly across the road and yell impotently at her. Mid Sunday afternoon the traffic was sparse which probably saved our lives because seat belts were non mandatory in 1960.
'Wow, he's a monster' I said nonchalantly reaching over and touching the pincer of an enormous shiny stag beetle which filled the box. 'Isn't he a bit uncomfortable in there' I asked without engaging my brain. 'Probably' said the budding entomologist as

he tipped him out on my hand. I knew this was a make or break moment and watched the look of glee turn to disappointment as I failed to react.

'It would be kinder to let him go' I told the little provoker as I offered the beetle back to him. Thus was my first encounter with Mark's wild life enthusiasm.

It was to be the first of many.

~~~~~

ABOUT THE AUTHOR

Bernadette writes;
I was born, bread and buttered in Summerhill a hard living area in Dublin. Being north of the Liffey we were 'real Dubliners'. By the mid 40's our Georgian and Regency terraces were advancing into decaying tenements but our wide streets were relatively traffic free and provided us children with an enviable freedom. They also provided hard-pressed Mammy's with hours of peace and quiet because apart from feeding any open beak that darkened the doorway the only time they saw their offspring was when they did a head count at bedtime. Even then it was not uncommon to find a cuckoo in the nest and one of your brood being scrubbed clean by a neighbour!

By my 18th year I knew that I was part of a generation whose future would be on a foreign shore. Ireland, an impoverished country with a dismal economic environment and De Valera's deeply conservative theocratic government would not be able to meet either our aspirations or expectations in the furtherance of a career. Our exodus was rationalized by many families as a temporary expedient until things improved at home but I was realistic enough to know that my exile would be a long one. Early in the New Year of 1957 I 'took the boat' to start my nurse training in London's East End. Half a century later, after a long career in Public Health Nursing, and despite having Gypsy feet I have settled into retirement here.